Why the Rich

Get Richer

The Secrets to Cash Flowing

Apartments

By

Corey Peterson

Dedication

I dedicate this book to my wonderful companion and best friend, who happens to be my wife, Shelley. You looked at a used car salesman and saw a diamond in the rough. Not only have you always believed in me, you believed when I couldn't believe in myself. As a devoted companion, you took the time to polish me with your tender words of encouragement and unfailing belief in me, even after I failed time and time again. You have always picked me back up, dusted me off and sent me back out to fearlessly try again. The brilliance and radiance I have today is only because of you. And through your eyes, one would never be able to see my flaws. My Love, words will never be able to tell you how utterly and totally you have completed me and made me whole. You're my soulmate, best friend, and lover. It has been my honor and privilege to do life with you.

Table of Contents

Introduction

Did you ever play Monopoly as a kid? I remember the games my family would play as we were growing up and how much fun we had. The rules were simple. Get a monopoly, build houses and then finally trade them in for hotels that charge the big bucks.

In my younger years, I didn't have a clue that in the future as a seasoned investor buying cash flowing, multi-family apartments, I would be playing monopoly in real life. Nor did I know I'd be making "the big bucks." I also didn't know the game I play now would be just as fun and exciting as back then. Finally, I didn't know the battle scars I'd endure from making mistakes along the way. If I have learned anything, it's that real estate is constantly changing. With the increase of technology, it's changing faster than ever. Not only is real estate changing, but how people want to make a living is changing as well.

I have sat across from hundreds of very high income, successful people looking for ways to get out of the rat race. When I talk with these individuals, I hear many of the same things. Doctors, dentists, chiropractors and health care professionals are frustrated with health care being forced down their throats, all while seeing shrinking profit margins. They know if they don't go to work, they won't get paid. So, each day they go to work (like zombies), going through life yet not really living. I've seen business owners make huge profits, but then tell me how much they work and how unhappy they are. They want nothing more than to retire and enjoy life again. Then there are those who make money doing good, but don't trust the stock market anymore. They are looking for alternative ways to make their money grow. I'm convinced most people are looking for two things: *time and money*. People who tend to have a lot of time seem to not always have a lot of money. Those who have a lot of money, tend to not have much time. The question then becomes, how do you have both?

I believe that real estate can help one acquire both. In fact, I believe most people reading this book want to be doing real estate in some way, shape or form. Here is the problem: most wealthy people are incredibly busy. They are usually business owners or high-level corporate professionals. Because these types of people are very focused on what they do, they lack the time it takes to learn the ins and outs of the real estate market.

They really want to, but cannot seem to ever get there.

This is where my company steps in. We have spent thousands of hours mastering what we do in the real estate industry. We buy apartment complexes (in good markets) that provide cash flow and back-end profits. This is what busy professionals desire and need. We do this using a unique process which allows everyone to win in an asset class they do not build anymore.

When I talk with business owners and high net worth professionals, I tend to see a common theme. If I asked them to look at their net worth and tell me where their money is parked, the answer would surprise you. Did you know that most people's money is not parked in cash? Think about it; where is most of your savings right now? If you are like most, it's probably in your Individual Retirement Account (IRA), or some qualified account such a 401K. Why is this? Because we have been conditioned to put our money in these vehicles. They are a great place to put money, as it can grow tax-deferred and tax-free if you have a Roth IRA.

Now for the mind-blowing question. Did you know you can invest in real estate using your IRA or qualified account? The answer is yes, you can.

Why the Rich Get Richer

The reason you may not know this is because most people open accounts with firms they see on TV – think Merrill Lynch, Morgan Stanley, etc. In these types of brokerages, you can only invest in what the brokerage has allowed their financial advisors to sell. Usually, this consists of all paper assets - CD's, bonds, stocks, mutual funds, etc. When you ask an advisor to invest in real estate, they will offer you a REIT, Real Estate Investment Trust. Which, by the way, is still a paper asset.

What you want is a Self-Directed IRA company that will be the fiduciary for you and allow you to invest in alternative investments, like real estate. By using your IRA money that has a longer-term outlook and making it grow with consistent returns, your wealth can grow leaps and bounds.

Let me take you on an educational journey of how I made it in real estate and how I have unlocked the secrets of creating massive cash flow for my investors by buying apartment buildings. I think you will find the stories fun and exciting! By the end of the book, you may want to get some yourself! Paradise awaits you in these chapters. Be bold, read on as I open up the playbook sharing how I operate and control multi-million-dollar assets using other people's money. And, most importantly, how I help them earn a great return on their investment.

Corey Peterson

Why the Rich Get Richer

Chapter 1

Getting Fired Was My Salvation

I grew up in a small town in Missouri that had a population of less than 18,000. In fact, that was the town. Our house was located 25 minutes out in the country. My parents, four siblings and I lived in a small two-bedroom house on a 180-acre farm.

We learned the value of hard work on that farm. We learned how to pick rock. We learned how to bale hay. More importantly, we learned the lessons that only someone raised in the country would know. You can take a country boy, put him into the city and he's fine. But bring a city kid to the country and well, it's miserable for him. Although we had a farm and we raised beef cattle, my father was a roofer by trade. He owned his own roofing business and taught me the trade. As a matter of fact, as my grandpa had taught my father that trade as well, I was in line to be a 3rd generation roofer. What my father really taught me was I never wanted to be a roofer. The man working up on a roof was not who

Why the Rich Get Richer

I knew my father to be – I did not know that guy. All I knew was, on the roof, he was the absolute boss and my job was to make sure I never made him look bad. That meant working extremely hard and doing the best job I could every single time. Although life was tough living in the country, to this day, I would not trade those lessons and gifts I learned in my youth.

For Dad's roofing lesson, it was a wise one. You see, I'm a country boy at heart. I believe in waving to others as you drive down the road. I believe you help out your fellow man in need. I believe in doing what's right. I also believe in doing what I say I'll do and speaking in plain English, without embellishment. In other words, get to the point and say what's on your mind.

In 2003, I had an incredible opportunity to go on a vacation that would ultimately change my life. My future wife and I flew to Hawaii with my mom and her husband, who had a home on the beach in Kauai - better known as "The Garden Island." This place was absolutely amazing. The home was right on the beach. You could run out into the back yard, walk over the berm, and WHAM! You were in the soft white sand watching the powerful ocean waves crash down. It gets better though - not only was the home right on the ocean, it was located on a cove. We walked around the cove early our first morning and I was astonished at what I saw - a fresh-water stream from the mountains above came rushing through and into the ocean. This place was something magical! I never could have dreamed how great this place was. This is probably why, to this day, it's my favorite vacation spot.

As I soak in the island, I look at my mom's husband, who I will call Bruce Wayne. I looked at Bruce and he didn't seem to have a care in this world. He was just there playing and enjoying life as Shelley and I were. When I took a closer look, he had nice cars in the garage, fine art in his home, and his phone was not ringing off the hook. He didn't seem to be worried about business. I knew then that I needed to ask Bruce what he did for a living. I saw he had the two things most people only dream of: time and money.

It took a while, but I was finally able to muster enough confidence to approach Bruce and ask him what he did for a living. When I asked, he simply looked at me and said, "Real Estate." Now, me being young and naïve, responded by saying, "so you're a realtor?" "No, No." Bruce said, "They work for me."

I left Hawaii and all I could think was that Bruce was indeed the BIG KAHUNA. He had time and money and lived by his own rules. I wanted that, but I just didn't know how to get it.

A year later, in 2004, I pick up a book that had been getting a lot of press and finally decided to read it. I wanted to understand what all the hype was about. The book was called "Rich Dad Poor Dad" by Robert Kiyosaki. This book changed my life forever. When I finished reading it, I knew exactly what Bruce Wayne was. He was a Real Estate Investor. I understood that he leveraged his money with bank money and bought cash flowing assets to put money into his pocket each month. I now understood why Bruce had so much time available. He set himself up to live on the cash flow from his business that bought multi-family apartments.

I now became obsessed with learning more. I would go into Barnes and Noble, peruse the Real Estate section and buy all the books I could find. I read books every day and night, seeing and learning the different strategies, strengthening my mind and crafting my plan. I knew what I wanted to do and finally in July of 2005, I created my flagship company Kahuna Investments LLC. It was aptly named because I wanted to be the

BIG KAHUNA!

Why the Rich Get Richer

I loved to read, and the books I read advised calling banks and talking to the Real Estate Owned (REO) departments. I opened the yellow pages and went to Credit Unions. I felt they were not as intimidating as the "big bad: corporate banks. There I found American Airlines Federal Credit Union at the top of the list. Nervously, I dialed the number and when the receptionist answered, I squeaked out something that sounded like, "Can I talk to the head of your REO department?" I ended up speaking to a woman named Holly. Holly was the head of the REO Department and she had properties available in Tulsa, Oklahoma. The books taught me to have cash available as a down payment. So, for operating capital, I took out a home equity line of credit. I bought my first two homes from Holly. I flipped them and made some money - $15,000 on one and $20,000 on the other.

I did so well I quit my job.

However, I soon found out that was a mistake. The next three properties I bought were rentals, and this was where I ran into my first real issue. *I ran out of money*. I put all the money I earned from the sale of the first two homes into my rental properties. I didn't have enough income to stay in the real estate business. Back to square one. I wanted to look for a new job that I could leverage for Real Estate. I accepted a job as a financial advisor. I knew if I did well in this position, the potential to earn a significant income was there. I could then show proof-of-income to banks in order for them to lend me money. During that process, we moved to Phoenix, Arizona. I enjoyed three years of selling securities in a great market. Then in 2008, it all changed for the worse; the market crashed. Not only did people's investments lose half their value, but in a years' time (in 2009) Phoenix real estate values dropped by half as well.

What happened next was my salvation. I had lost all desire to be a financial advisor. It seemed all the investments I made early on were in the gutter. Moreover, the people that came into my office were crying and scared to death. I really hated my job. So, when my boss scheduled a meeting with me, I knew there was a good chance I would be let go. I remember walking into the office, looking at my administrative assistant, and knowing the call had been made. She couldn't even look at me. I walked calmly into my office, sat down, and felt a moment of despair.

I couldn't believe it; I was going to get FIRED.

As my time as a financial advisor came to an end, an old desire burned back inside me. Somehow, while pursuing the game of stocks and bonds, I somehow had forgotten about real estate. As if awoken from a dream, I began to look around and saw real estate was on sale again.

It was on Sale BIG TIME....

I couldn't believe it - I had just been saved from being crushed in the real estate market by becoming a financial advisor. Shortly thereafter, I found myself on the other side with real estate prices at an all-time low.

Every book I had ever read all had a common theme. When the market is down, that is the best time to win. And win BIG in real estate. I had just been fired and was really struggling with what I should do next. Yet as I walked out of my office, I knew I couldn't just go home.

I took a short five-minute drive, arrived at Starbucks and ordered some hot coffee. It was time to figure things out. You see, I had this kid in my head that used to dream really big and wanted to win. It was that same good ol' country boy who knew he could do the hard work. He believed if he fully committed himself he could be great. But that kid was staring up at this older guy full of self-doubt. He was thinking about security, how the world worked, about supporting his family, and all the things that come along with being an adult. Suddenly, he wasn't so sure...

I was at a crossroads with myself. I knew what I wanted to do; I had known it for a very long time. I wanted to be like Bruce. I wanted time and money and freedom. I'm proud to say as I write this book, that the little kid kicked the crap out of the man and won the day.

It was in that moment that I made the most honest, noble, and courageous commitment to me. I vowed to myself that I was going to become a successful real estate investor. I made a commitment to MYSELF that I would never be defeated, and that I would never, ever quit. And although I didn't know exactly how I would get there, I left Starbucks with the resolve that I was going to make it in real estate or else. Now, all I had to do was tell my wife...

Training and Getting Started

Once I committed, I knew I needed real education. I went to a Rich Dad's Real Estate training program, a Robert Kiyosaki event. It was there that I met Bob Norton. Bob was offering a system called "KISS Flipping" – "Keep It Simple Stupid" Flipping. I invested in his course, and immediately learned he was different. Up to this point, all the books I had read taught old and out-of-date systems. By the time I was reading about their strategies, they had changed. But KISS FLIPPING was internet based, a strategy that was working. Bob became my first mentor and showed me how to use the Multiple Listing Service (MLS) to find Real Estate Owned (REO) properties and short sales. I took that system and blew it up.

Bob offered "50/50" deals - he would provide all necessary funding, but I had to find deals and manage the rehab. If the deals met his specific criteria, he would split profits with me 50/50. Once Bob shared the outline of an acceptable 50/50 deal and showed me how to find them, I quickly became one of his top guys. At one point, we had almost $1 million "on the street." Things were going so well that Bob's brother wanted a piece of the business. However, this meant I was once again, out of a job.

Back in crisis mode, what do I do? My work with Bob had been my only source of income, I was performing well, and I enjoyed doing it. However, there was a silver lining. Bob had taught me how to lock up and control deals. He'd also taught me to take videos and pictures of every deal I ever did. I found this gave me "street cred" in the market. I took that information, created a marketing piece (with video links) and brought it to my local REIA (Real Estate Investors Association). I presented myself as a Real Estate Wholesaler and my deals where PHAT. I soon found two multi-millionaires who wanted to buy my properties. We ended up having a great working relationship.

Eventually I smartened up and raised my first piece of private capital… totally by accident.

By working the 50/50 deals with Bob and wholesaling my own deals, building my business, I had built up a solid wholesaling track record. I had finally convinced myself I knew what I was doing. I found a glitch though – I was taking small fees on the wholesale side, yet giving away the big profits to the investors. I knew my deals were good because, in fact, I tracked them even after my investors sold them. I put in a lot of work finding the deals, yet they made most of the profit. It was clear that I needed to find a way to earn the big profit and pay someone else the wholesaling fee.

I knew I didn't have a great deal of cash, yet knew that was what was required to do more real estate deals. How could I convince others to "give me their money" so I could financially help us both? And more importantly, I could pay that small fee out in interest, thus making the big money for myself. Unfortunately for me, I had no idea how to do this. I grew up with little means and although I had learned the financial markets as an advisor, I was still afraid to ask others for money. What I didn't know then, that I know now, is that I wasn't asking people for their money - I had a real opportunity to share.

I raised my first piece of private money totally by accident. I played racquetball with one of my old investors (we will call him Carl). Carl was with me in my Financial Advisor days. This gentleman had most of his money tied up in investments called annuities. While they paid him cash flow, he could not get out of them. I didn't think he had any other available extra money. But, Carl did live in a retirement community and I figured he might know some people who would be interested. I told Carl that if he knew anyone looking to make some extra money, I could pay 12% and give a house as collateral against the loan. Carl played racquetball with me every Thursday and he had watched me grow my business. But I really didn't think he had any extra money, so I was asking Carl for help as a friend. After I gave Carl my spiel, he looked at me and said, "yeah, I'll see what I can do." That was that, and we went back to playing racquetball.

The next day I got a call from... guess who...???

You guessed it, Carl. He said, "Corey, do you still want to do that deal and pay 12%?" I replied, "Sure." I was so thrilled - Carl had found someone who was interested. I was "doing the happy dance." Then Carl proceeded to tell me, "Corey, I'm not sure if you know this, but my home is totally paid for. And if you are willing to pay 12% for money, I can borrow against my house at 3.2%. That means I can make a spread. Corey, how much money do you need?"

To that I replied, "Carl, I need $85,000 for the deal." Carl simply said, "Great. Where do you want me to send it?"

This question caught me off guard. You should understand, at this point,

I hadn't made the necessary arrangements to see the deal all the way through. I fumbled for a minute and let Carl know I'd have to get back with him. A couple days later, I made arrangements with my title company for Carl to wire his money to them. This marked a milestone in my career - my first deal with OPM "Other People's Money."

When this happened, all I can tell you is, I felt like Clark Kent running down the alley pulling his suit out to reveal Superman. I had never dreamed of other people giving me their money. I was humbled that someone trusted me enough to make their money grow. It was an awesome feeling!

The Money is in the Money

I learned to perfect the capital raising business, and a very valuable lesson. I thought that real estate was "where it's at" and in a way, it was. What I have come to realize is, the money is not in real estate - the money is in the money. You can find all the deals you want, but without any money to buy them, you will always settle for that smaller paycheck. Once I found this to be true, I began to seek out mentors who were raising lots of capital.

I needed a guide for taking people's money. I created a "private money program guide" with the purpose of educating investors on how my company worked and how we invested people's money. To get a copy of my guide, go to **www.WhyTheRichGetRicher.net/downloads**. I taught my investors how to play the bank and lend my company money to do deals. Another piece I created was my Credibility Kit. Using all the videos and pictures in my portfolio, I compiled all my previous wholesale and rehab deals. I then created a document detailing my expertise. In other words, I could now tell a story about how I used other people's money to buy real estate, and more importantly make it grow. It didn't take long before I realized I needed to be in a leadership role. With leadership in mind, I created an REIA (Real Estate Investor Association) called "East Valley Investors Club" - which still exists today. I teach others what I do in my wholesale single-family business. This, in turn, helps me with credibility and notoriety, which helps to raise more private money. People with money want to do business with other successful people. It didn't take long before I had millions of dollars on the street working, doing flips and rehabs.

Shifting Gears

My business flipping single-family homes was going nicely. I had lots of private money lined up and I was able to find deals using the MLS. That was until the market began to change. You see for me, I had only learned one way to find deals. Remember how Bob Norton taught me to find deals on the MLS with REOs and short sales? He'd never taught me the art of marketing. So, when the short sales and REO became harder and harder to find, it was like "Houston, we have a problem." It became clear I needed to find another way to source single family homes and do so quickly. Yet, I had something a little bigger in mind. I knew my private investors were counting on me to be able to place their investments and make their money grow. I had a hunch my next idea would be awesome.

Big Deals Big Money

When I first started investing in 2005, I vividly remember driving by apartment complexes and saying to myself, "I wish I could own one of those." Really, at that point in my life, wishing meant "it's a pipe dream." But here I was in a market where I had lots of private money behind me and was driving by apartments saying the same darn thing. I wish... I wish...I wish...

But things changed the day I reframed my mindset and hit the reset button in my brain. Instead of *wishing* I could buy an apartment complex, I asked myself a simple question: "How *could I buy* an apartment complex?" By framing it as a question, all the power in my brain started firing. The next question to myself was, "Corey, what do you know about apartments or multi-family buildings?" I answered truthfully and said, "not much." I asked myself another question, "Where could you get some information on multi-family apartments?" Once again, without hesitation, my brain gave me the answer: Go to the bookstore and see what's out there.

Next thing I knew, I purchased seven books from, you guessed it, AMAZON, and started to take in all the information I could. I was looking for an author I could relate to and help me understand the process. Unfortunately, it took me until book #7, the last book I read, to hit the jackpot. The book I'm referring to? "Multi-Family Millions," by Dave Lindahl. Dave owned more than 7,000 units and had a lot of knowledge. More importantly, Dave wrote in such a way that I could understand exactly what he was doing. I knew I needed to meet him.

While I wanted to invest in his course, I made it clear I wouldn't make the purchase unless I was able to personally have lunch with Dave. I wanted to do my due diligence.

It's important to do so and not be influenced by a flashy presentation or one 30-minute speech.

So, I flew to Boston, where Dave lives, from my home in Phoenix just to have lunch and get to know him as a person. He's honest, hardworking, came from nothing like I did, and his family works in his business. He's a stand-up guy, has taught me the ropes, and has been a true mentor. We recently did an interview discussing the value of mentorship. To see this interview, go to **www.WhyTheRichGetRicher.net/DavidLindahl**.

Dave taught me how to underwrite, locate and find cash flowing deals.

More than that, he showed me how to properly structure the deals.

After doing countless underwritings on potential apartment deals, I felt it was finally time to actually bring one in. I still had the huge problem of millions of dollars in private monies that needed to be placed, yet no single-family deals to put it in. I knew it was only a matter of time before I found a deal that made sense. And wouldn't you know it, a deal fell in my lap. Well, not actually - here's what happened and how I did my first apartment deal.

After lots of searching and talking with many brokers in areas in which I wanted to invest, I was getting a decent amount of deals to look at and underwrite. I just hadn't found the perfect one. Since this was to be my first shot out of the gate, I knew I needed a deal with a lot of "meat on the bone." But how I found my first deal surprised even me.

By now, I was an avid fan of Dave Lindahl's and I had been taking all of his courses. I attended his 'Manage the Manager' event in Rhode Island. Upon arrival, I told myself I was going to do things differently. Instead of being busy, trying to network and find other like-minded people, I specifically wanted to see if I could catch a deal. So, when the opportunity presented itself, I stood up tall and from the back of the room, I belted out, "My name is Corey Peterson with Kahuna Investments. I have a crap ton of cash and I'm looking for deals." By the end of the weekend, I was able to see every deal other investors had. I had managed to flip the script and didn't even mean to. I now had investors chasing me, wanting me to give them money.

On a quick side note, I'm going to repeat something. *The Money is in the Money.* Remember this...the money is always patient, never acts in haste, is always prudent and always demands the best possible outcome. He who has the money, makes the rules.

Why the Rich Get Richer

As I stated, I looked at many deals that weekend. But one deal, in particular, really stood out. It was a 144-unit deal in Greenville, South Carolina called Lionsgate. The price tag on this property was $3.2 million. I really liked the economics of the Carolinas and felt this property had all the right things wrong.

It was an REO that suffered from bad personnel and management, as well as a lot of deferred maintenance. Deferred maintenance is a nice way of saying the current owner let things go downhill and didn't upkeep the property. These issues were all very fixable and I knew it could be done quickly. Even better, the group that had the deal under contract was in a pickle. They had $100,000 hard - meaning if they did not close, they would lose the money. Not only was their money hard, the group only had 15 days to close. The amount of money needed to fully fund the deal was around $1.4 million. Not only was I able to negotiate a 75% ownership stake in the deal, I also brought in all the money for it as well. I eventually bought out the investors and now own it 100%. But it gets better. As I write this book, we just listed Lionsgate on the market for $9 million. Pretty cool, right?

Once I learned the formula, I simply repeated the process over and over again. Find deals, fund them and operate the properties for cash flow. It's a fairly simple process, but it takes a great team to properly execute it. And fortunately for my company, we have the best team out there.

Why the Rich Get Richer

Chapter 2

Perfecting the Process

This book is for the 40+-year-old individual or business level executive who earns a considerably high income and wants their money to work as hard as they do. One of today's financial problems is that few people truly understand the stock market. At times, it goes up and down for what appears to be no reason. What I have come to find out is most investors hate the volatility of the stock market. I've also found that many investors have most of their money in qualified accounts like IRA and Roth IRA, leading them to believe their only investment options are stocks, bonds and mutual funds. Basically, whatever their broker offers and suggests – paper assets. Most people are not aware they can use their IRA money to invest in real estate. When we show people how, it blows their minds.

Remember, people don't trust the stock market. Furthermore, they realize what will happen once the Baby Boomers begin to cash in their retirement funds and start drawing them down. Suddenly, there's going to be a tremendous demand for liquid cash, which will really hurt the stock market.

What I love about our business model is that our investors become owners with us in the deal. More importantly, they can visit and touch the building. It's not pie in the sky. Most people who are savvy investors know they should have some real estate in their portfolio. We allow a shortcut to the source.

With that said, many of our new investors have been referrals from past clients who are happy with what we've done for them. It's not uncommon for someone to call me and say he's interested in finding out about the opportunities we offer.

When this happens, the first thing I like to do is to find out what kind of investor they are and what they want to achieve. I've learned over the years that you must listen.

I've seen people get pushed into deals that may not have been what they're looking for. Situations such as this can be alleviated by having a simple conversation. You need to know people's risk tolerance. Have they done any prior real estate deals? What's the investor's time horizon? Can they stay in a deal for up to 5 years? Are they seeking yield or are they seeking cash flow? I think most people want a little of both. Most investors want to make a solid return that pays cash flow and provides a chance to make a little more upside. I have found that almost everyone loves mailbox money and loves the idea of getting checks every quarter.

As I have great conversations with potential investors, I'm also thinking to myself "do I want this person in my deal?" There's nothing worse than having a five-year professional relationship with someone you simply do not get along with or is the proverbial thorn in your side.

I've also come to realize that Kahuna is not always the right fit for everybody. Sometimes it's easier to tell people "no" in the beginning, before we get too far along in the process. It saves everybody a lot of time, headaches, trials and tribulations. I've had some investors with large amounts of money to spend that expect huge returns. They've been conditioned to take on very risky deals and are chasing a huge yield. We're just not that shop.

What we try to achieve in our deals is the consistency factor. We base them on the criteria that people have a basic need for food, clothing and shelter. We like to do what I call the "shelter mission." Our approach is to be very systematic and straightforward. We like to find a "working man's" type of apartment complex. These apartments were built between 1970 and the early 1990's. They don't have flashy amenities the new complexes have, but they do service a large portion of the population. I believe that people, regardless of income, will always gravitate to the best possible housing within their budget. Our goal is to make the apartments we operate the best in their class, pulling the best tenants in that particular price range. People want clean, affordable living. If we can deliver that, and shorten someone's commute, that's a recipe for success. That's our objective.

The first call with a potential client is a preliminary conversation to see if we are a good fit for one another. In the current market, there are many more people seeking this type of investment than there are good, safe, solid investments. We want to make sure that personality-wise, the person is a good fit with us.

The next step is to look at their current position - not just financially, but physically and emotionally. We want to ensure that, not only is the investment a good fit for their current portfolio, and the risk tolerance is right, but their expectations are reasonable and achievable.

Finally, we want to know if the investor is educated and accredited who is hands-on, or will they need significant education before we proceed?

Once we know the investor's basic status, and they have filled out our Accredited Investors Form*, we then send out our Credibility Kit. Remember I had one for my single-family flips? I also have one for my multi-family business.

*indicates they have a net worth of $1 million or more (not including their personal home) or earn an annual income of at least $250K a year.

The Kahuna Credibility Kit outlines the type of properties we target - which sizes and locations. It contains information about our process, as well as our team. It also shows a potential investor what we own and operate. Our goal is to make sure we can show you, without a doubt, that we are indeed experts at what we do. I've spent over 1,000 hours getting my education in the business and feel I've mastered the game. Let me be clear, though. I've mastered single-family flips, single-family wholesale and multi-family apartments. In those areas, I'm very skilled and knowledgeable. Yet, if you asked me to take on a commercial office or retail space, I would tell you "I'm not your man." What I've learned over time is that experts make money. In the areas I've just shared, I'm that expert. I've also learned the generalist usually makes excuses, and that's the reason why I won't engage in business deals other than those within my core competencies.

Not only will I send out our Credibility Kit, but if we are in the process of working a deal, I will send details on it as well. We call this our Property Packet - a brochure explaining our investment and how it works. Of course, there are times we're not going to have deals working. Our goal then is to have enough people raising their hands saying they "want in" on our upcoming deal. Since our model focuses on quality deals, we may only do 3-4 deals each year.

These apartments are typically 100+ units and are big projects. Most of the time, the deals we buy require large amounts of capital in order to improve the property. To ensure we are not stressing our systems, we operate at somewhat of a slower pace. We function at this rate because if we moved much faster, we would be sacrificing quality control. When you're dealing with other people's money, it's just not worth it.

Our goal is to make sure our management team can get into the property. It is vital for us to do our due diligence on the front end, so we know what we need to move forward. This is important as we work to get our management team set up and ready to properly make moves to our property before we even start.

Why the Rich Get Richer

Another reason we choose to only do 3-4 projects a year is because it helps us, from an operational standpoint, function more efficiently. We don't want to begin a new project until we've got proper stabilization in place for existing projects. This encompasses personnel, as an integral part of the entire process. We are able to get the property moving in the right direction, toward achieving our desired goal. When we take over a new property, it's a bit like having a baby. We may be working long hours checking off to-do list items, as well as repairing many deferred maintenance projects. Once we know the property is on the right track, it's then time for us to find another.

Another reason we don't scale up too much is because my wife and I are typically the biggest investors in any of our deals. We are personally invested in making sure every deal is successful. Not only is our money in play, of course, other people's money is as well. I personally feel other people's money is more important than my own, and therefore we choose to put our investors ahead of ourselves. I don't think everybody does this, but I think they should.

The proverbial "golden goose" in what Kahuna does with apartments is raising capital. By far, this is the most important part of our operation. Our priority lies in taking care of what we call "the money" - the people who bring us their capital. Number one – we are the guardians of their money. Number two - a grower of their money.

Our investors usually get a preferred return based upon the cash flow of our deal. This means, they get first dip out of the bucket. We don't pay ourselves until our investors make that preferred return.

The fact that our investors bring us referrals proves we are doing things the right way. In fact, most of our new capital comes from referrals in the networks of people currently invested in our deals. Additionally, most current investors usually want to be included in our next ones.

They love the experience and begin to see for themselves how it really works for them. They like seeing the mailbox money! Who wouldn't? If you want to learn how you can earn some mailbox money for yourself, go to **www.WhyTheRichGetRicher.net/Income** to let us know you're interested. We will send you our Credibility Kit and start the process. Accredited investors only, please.

Doing Due Diligence

Once we have a deal in place and have qualified our investor, we then send out our Property Packet. At this point, we typically have the property under contract and a minimum of $100,000 in earnest money secured. Remember, the Property Packet lays out the foundation of how we foresee the deal going, as well as how we need to operate in order to increase value. It also includes a 5-year conservative underwriting projection. This takes into account our experience in operations, as well as shows our estimated investor returns.

When we lock a property in contract, there's usually a period of time allowed for inspections. This is the "due diligence" period. It's the time we take to review the property's total condition. There are two stages: physical due diligence and financial due diligence. During physical due diligence, we do things like check electric and A/C systems, plumbing, overall condition of each unit, the outside of the building, as well as a roof inspection. We then obtain estimates for any work that may need to be done. This is all done before we make a purchase decision so as to ensure we will meet our targeted rehab budgets. To ensure a comprehensive overview of the property, we use a combination of licensed inspectors and a head maintenance supervisor. After the physical stage, we then start financial due diligence. Although I'm referring to these as two separate stages, we normally have two teams working simultaneously.

Why the Rich Get Richer

In the financial due diligence stage, we look at and verify all property numbers. We look at each tenant and review their lease jacket. Kahuna closely examines each tenant's credit score, payment history and criminal record. In addition, we identify tenants who may no longer meet our criteria. When these leases are up for renewal, Kahuna reserves the right to deny. The next step is to review utility expenditures such as electricity, water, sewer and waste. We look specifically at historical figures to ensure they match the seller provided financials. Our job is to know where all money comes from and goes to. We also search for expenses that can be eliminated. You'd be surprised how many apartment owners are overpaying for the same items we get for much less. This inspection process is typically a $10,000 expense. I will tell you, it's worth every penny. In this business, you do NOT want surprises. It's always better to measure twice and only cut once.

In our packet, we provide several useful pieces of information – unit quantity, unit mix (one bedroom, two, etc.), and where we see opportunity. Also, and I think more importantly, we provide what we view as the economic situation of not only the property, but the city in which the property is located. We need to ensure we will be operating in a city large enough to make sense. We look for indicators, such as a local airport with major carriers, universities/colleges, large hospitals, and a strong job market. Surprisingly, we try to stay away from major markets. We prefer submarkets and usually find better opportunities. As far as economic indicators, we look for a growing workforce. This means jobs are coming into the area, not leaving. This is very important.

As we consider an area, we also look at crime statistics. Typically, women are the decision makers when it comes to where their families live. Selecting areas with low crime rates is very important to them. The Kahuna threshold is a crime rate below both the state average and within the property's zip code. Another factor we take into consideration is the traffic count from the nearest major streets and thruways. It's important to know how many people regularly drive those roads. After all, they are future prospects.

It all circles back to our main idea: when we can provide affordable, clean housing, and shorten someone's commute, we win every time. In short, we do our due diligence and that's how we anticipate maintaining occupancy in our properties.

At this point in the process, our investors have a property packet in hand, and they have reviewed the deal and more than likely have many questions. They want to understand our plan to create value. How will we increase rent? How will we repair and update the property making it clean and nice, yet still maximize profitability? That's usually done in a one-on-one discussion. We prefer face-to-face, but many of our investors are out of state, so we defer to technology by using a webinar format. This ensures both parties are looking at the same thing and are actively learning about the deal.

When we send a property packet to a potential investor, we usually already have a fairly accurate picture of what improvements need to be completed. But sometimes, we miss things. For this reason, once we are officially under contract, we spend approximately $10,000 on a formal inspection. We closely examine the health of the entire property, both physical and financial.

For one property in particular, it was raining the day we were on site. We saw eight active leaks. The seller had to have known about these leaks; however, they were never disclosed. Since we had hired a skilled roofer to inspect properties, we found the leaks. This left us with decisions to make. It's not uncommon for sellers not to disclose things. We see it often and therefore we rely on our process. A complete roof replacement on that project would essentially kill the deal. Luckily for us we had a plan.

Knowing we had roof leaks, our team secured multiple bids and told the seller, regardless if we purchased his property or not, it would be in his best interests to repair the problem. We received multiple bids and could show, beyond a doubt, we could not incur the cost of a repair deferment. Our due diligence allowed us to obtain a $175,000 roof. With that credit, we could still make our numbers work and knew our property would soon have a brand-new roof. If we hadn't secured that credit, the deal would more than likely have dissolved. At that point, it was just not workable; our numbers would tell us so. Remember, we were unaware of the roof problem and therefore hadn't budgeted for it. The actual cost of replacing the roof was $225,000, so the $175,000 went a very long way. Without the seller credit, our numbers would not have allowed for us to incur the cost risk of installing a new roof. Sometimes we plan on doing deals, but when things go wrong, we have learned through experience to not force it. That's how you get into trouble. We have learned to trust our process and not waver from it.

Once we finish Due Diligence (inspection period) and have negotiated with the seller for anything we were unhappy with, it is at that point we go hard. Hard means our earnest money is now at risk and we need to close. Finally, we are ready to create our Private Placement Memorandum - a document used to pool capital together and begin to work with our investors to fund the deal. This document reviews the property and its operation in detail and is regulated by the Security and Exchange Commission. It's prepared by a lawyer and costs between $15,000 to $20,000 to prepare. When we are running the property, the PPM and its rules are what guide us when it comes to distributions, payments, etc.

Once we have received the money, we set the closing date. Next, we close on the property and the real work begins!! Operations – this is where most investors fail. Unfortunately, they do not understand the complexity of projects nor do they have the necessary knowledge. We also have a few special tricks we implement in our units. I'll talk about them in a later chapter. Just know I'm going to reveal some Wudan Shaolin Monk Kung Fu in the way my team operates. It's truly first class.

The only real question is, do you want to learn more about being one of our investors in our deals?

Go to **www.WhyTheRichGetRicher.net/downloads** to get my Credibility Kit and learn more about us.

Chapter 3

Not Every Investment is Perfect

One of the deals I'm most proud of is a 144- unit complex, currently on the market, that Kahuna purchased in 2011. The best part of that deal is we bought it for $3.2 million. The property is located in Greenville, South Carolina. While Greenville is not a huge city, it has a commercial airport and is home to some large manufacturing facilities. The BMW plant is there, as well as a couple of tire manufacturers. If you recall, I talked about this deal in chapter one. When we bought this deal, it was 70% occupied, an REO – a bank-owned property.

Not only did it have an occupancy problem, it also had a huge drug problem. In fact, when we brought the City of Malden Police to the property, we allowed them to utilize a free unit to police the area. Our initial thought was to simply implement a name change for the property. It had a reputation... Experience told us with name changes, they just don't work. You can put lipstick on a pig, but it's still a pig. The only way that we were going to change this property was to change it from the inside out.

The first thing we did was evict the undesirable tenants. We were able to issue violations which allowed us to legally ask them to leave. Next, we had Mauldin Police "lend us" their drug dogs. That was fun! We posted a notice on all units informing tenants the Mauldin Police would be using our property to conduct training for their drug dogs. Can you believe we had three units clear out in the middle of the night?! That helped tremendously and eliminated the drug problem. Once we started actively managing our property and letting all tenants know things were changing for the better, everyone got on board. Tenants began to seek us out to thank us for creating a safer environment for their families.

Why the Rich Get Richer

One of the most important things we've learned in this business is you're either going to train the tenants or your tenants are going to train you. That's called Active Management. We actively managed our property. We kept our heads up by watching what was going on and then we implemented a rehab. We've spent almost half a million dollars in rehab for this property. Not only did we replace the roofs, we rehabbed the interior with new flooring, new paint, cabinets, and other finishes. By cleaning and updating the property, we made it more acceptable and affordable.

Next, our focus shifted to the property's grounds. The grounds were overgrown and untidy, therefore we were attracting sloppy, lazy, and undesirable tenants. This is very common. There were no regulations regarding tree growth and maintenance so trees and hedges were out of control. It made the property an eyesore. It's not difficult to find what is desirable. If you drive to the newest apartment complexes, you can find what your landscaping should look like. We "creatively borrow" ideas from other successful complexes on ways to add value to our property at a sensible cost. On this property, we brutally trimmed back on the landscaping. By year two it looked awesome.

We now have this property listed for $9 million. This price is wholly justified; we have consistently increased rental income, improved the property and our tenant base.

We tripled our value by creating a healthy cash flow and are selling because we can "cash out" of the HOT South Carolina market allowing us to reinvest in another property in another up-and-coming market. Truth be told, it's hard for me to want to sell a cash-flowing property. Normally, we have a 5-6-year hold period before we refinance to repay our investors and still retain the asset. Yet at times, we've sold other properties to move into markets that have tons of potential. We do this so our investors can have big paydays.

Why the Rich Get Richer

Even though this unit is a tremendous success, it doesn't always work out that way. Kahuna purchased a 70-unit apartment complex in Tucson, Arizona. Comparatively to other properties, since I live in Phoenix, I considered this "my backyard." As is procedure, I did the appropriate due diligence and therefore thought it would be a good, solid deal. However, there was something I didn't count on – the ineptitude of my previous management company.

You have to keep in mind, most of our properties are located on the East coast or in the Southeast region of the country. Even though this particular one was in my backyard, I still hired my Atlanta-based management company to oversee the Tucson property. Unfortunately, they were horrible at it. They were doing great in South Carolina and other states in the region, but this one they just couldn't effectively manage.

This was a smaller property, only 70 units. It only supported two staff members – a Property Manager and a Maintenance Manager. I have found when only two people are working onsite, there must be a very effective management company actively overseeing the staff. Many times, when the Property Manager and Maintenance Manager befriend one another, they tend to leave the property unattended. They work out a system to "cover each other's' backs." Or at least they think they do. It wasn't long before tenants were calling to inform us they were unable to pay rent because no one was at the office to accept payment.

I made the decision to fire the east coast management company, then had a revolutionary idea. I knew I was capable of running and managing this property. Of course, as soon as I implemented the change, the property had a major sewer problem. This repair required digging thirty feet deep into concrete floors to replace the old rusted-through galvanized pipes. It was a complete mess!

I struggled to manage the staff and simultaneously maintain our high standards. Unfortunately, the property began to slip. I finally threw in the towel and hired a well-respected, local Tucson apartment management company, MEB. I learned a hard lesson from this one.

MEB came in and immediately started to turn the property around. We made virtually no money for eighteen month, or at best, a small return. We were only able to make a few payments to our investors. It was then we collectively decided it was time to release the property. I personally took a $70,000 loss on this deal, simply so I could pay out my investors. I was not contractually obligated to ensure each investor came out "whole." However, that's how I operate – I do the right thing.

We were able to get back their principal investment, as well as a small amount of interest. Let me share with you: when you operate with integrity, guess what happens? When we were unable to provide our investors the return we had hoped for, I felt horrible. I made mistakes that were truly mine, and ultimately, it cost our investors. However, I made sure to maintain constant communication with them, even when the information wasn't positive. The reality is, not every investment is perfect. It's just not.

What brings me pride and happiness is seventy percent of the Tucson investors are still with me. The ones who were first to go never returned. Yet the ones who experienced other deals with me were happy to invest again.

It's a Learning Process

One of the many things this experience taught me was I would never again make the choice to self-manage a property. I'm thankful for the learning opportunity. Over the years, I've seen almost every way people can cheat and steal money. I think, at one point or another, it has all happened to me. I've seen maintenance men leave and take expensive tools, like high dollar HVAC tools and power washer equipment, with them. I realized Property Managers have their own way to take rent paid in cash, which ends up in their pockets instead of Kahuna bank accounts! Better yet, I learned a boyfriend sometimes gets a free apartment, even though in our system it shows the unit as vacant! My eyes are wide open now.

It took a good six months wrestling with self-managing properties before I realized that approach was not for me. Don't get me wrong, I learned some very valuable lessons. I learned what to do and more importantly, what not to do. You learn what works and what doesn't. Some of the best experiences in life are lessons not on what you CAN do; but more on what you shouldn't do. Just because you can doesn't mean you should. Through the process of learning, you figure out that which you are best.

Learning I should never self-manage was a difficult lesson. Having those conversations with investors was certainly tough. Admitting you made a mistake is a very humbling task. But I'm grateful I made those choices. I could look the investors in their eye and say, "You know I took care of you. I made it right." For them to look back and say, "You know what? We appreciate that, Corey, and we're still with you," meant a lot. I honestly thought I'd never see those investors again. I thought none of them would ever come back and Kahuna was done. That goes to show when you operate with integrity and do the right thing, people understand. They would much rather you be upfront with them.

I know for certain the stock market is not a perfect investment option either. And I promise, you'll never get a call from the New York Stock Exchange or NASDAQ.

I take a personal interest in the investors who participate in my deals. I want to know them as people, as well as have them know me. It's a team effort and I make every effort to effectively communicate operational updates and how we are performing.

It is crucial to make sure an investment deal is the right fit for both parties. When you decide to bring on an investor, you've made a choice that will be with you for the next five years. We better like them, and they need to like us.

It's got to be about more than just money.

Chapter 4

Long Distance Property Management

After the experience in Tucson and issues with the management company not having the ability to go from region to region, I began an exhausting task of compiling the team I have today. You see, being able to successfully manage properties from a distance is really the key. A question I am often asked is "how do we manage from afar?" How does someone who lives in Phoenix, operate effectively when most of their properties are on the East Coast? How do we do accomplish that? The answer is "THE TEAM" and I have built a fantastic one. The bad taste in my mouth from the terrible loss in Tucson greatly affected me – I knew I'd never taste that again.

I realized most of our properties, more than likely, would not be in my Phoenix backyard. The capital rates are so low that most investors are betting on appreciation. That has never been my game. I'm into sexy cash flow, Big Kahuna style. Finding and interviewing multiple management companies was a daunting task encompassing six states. I was looking for the proverbial needle in the haystack. I needed a company with impeccable systems and training and also had the experience and capacity to grow. I found that needle, and wouldn't you know, the referral came from one of my grade school friends. He reached out via Facebook, yet had no idea I was searching for a management company. He did, however, want to connect me with some property manager friends of his in Columbia, Missouri. He could not stop talking about how good they were. Long story short, they are now the only company that manages my apartments. In fact, I give them a piece of my equity as well.

One of the problems I had was I felt no management company would ever care as much about a property as I did. My father offered fantastic insight one day, "Why don't you give them a reason to care." I didn't fully understand what pops meant and then he said, "Give them a piece of the profit. Align both your interests and those of your management company." My dad gave me a golden nugget of wisdom. I didn't want to be looking behind my back every month just waiting for the management company to rob me of money. By giving my management company part of the deal's back end, we were now perfectly aligned. Just as important, if not more so, this allowed both parties to operate at peak performance. I was able to focus on my gift - which is raising capital and working with investors. And the management team did what it's best at - operations.

Our operations and systems procedures are handled much differently than most companies. In a typical management company, a Regional Asset Manager is usually in charge of three to six apartment complexes. I find communication is unfortunately very one way. Meaning, the regional manager talks with the on-site property manager. The property manager then talks with the maintenance man and leasing professional. Leasing and maintenance departments only talk with the property manager. What happens with this setup is the staff feels isolated and alone. They could never get true support and morale suffers. I've seen this happen. We do it much differently with a fresh approach that screams TEAM.

Our management team embraces what I like to call a "tribe philosophy." Let me explain.

Creating the Tribe

Think back to American Indians. In a tribe, all young Indian braves would call every woman 'mother'. They all shared the joy of nurturing these young boys to manhood, teaching them along the way. Anyone brave never felt alone and always knew he could call on others for help. In that type of environment, you feel safe, and I think you learn better.

We feel that little Indian brave is our staff on property. Every member has a very important role, but they need help. The Kahuna management company at the corporate office comes in as the many mothers. We have people that only focus on one area of management and assist each brave involved with their task. For example, we have a 48-hour turn-around policy on a "make ready." This is a unit where either the tenant was evicted, or voluntarily moved out. Either way, in 48 hours the unit needs to be rent ready. At corporate, we have someone who is tasked with working this process. Since we usually know ahead of time when someone is scheduled to move out, the corporate mother works closely with his or her brave. Together, they make sure someone has been in the unit, and has taken stock of what will require repair. They help them open their eyes to see the little things that may otherwise go unnoticed. Then it's time to place parts orders. We need to ensure we have all the parts, tools, and whatever else is needed ready to go. This procedure is in place so when a tenant moves out, we are immediately in that unit, getting it back up to 'rent ready' status. We don't want to lose a precious rentable day.

Our brave is tasked with this big asset and his job is to make sure it's financially working. At the corporate level (at AFI) we have many Indian mothers looking at various aspects of our Indian's life. These could include financials, make-readies, maintenance reports, leasing statistics, and marketing efforts. There are department heads who help my team so the manager is not doing paperwork. He's not behind a desk with his head down. He's out there making a difference in our tenants' lives and in the lives of the people who work on our properties. He's out there meeting and greeting and making sure our standard of quality is maintained. This is important to us.

To effectively manage an apartment building you must track multiple KPI

(Key Performance Indicators). In fact, not only do they need to be tracked, each KPI needs to be assigned a meaning. By doing this, our team can communicate what "good" looks like and what is expected. One of the neat things we do with our management style is implement *Manager Mentors*. We use our seasoned veteran managers who have 'been there, done that' and are doing it now to train our new managers. We find this very helpful because you cannot pull something over on someone who's been there. Furthermore, because we set such an elevated level of excellence, we find at times new managers with old habits believe our expectations are unachievable. Utilizing the Manager Mentor, who indeed knows how the process works, allows collaboration and instills a new set of beliefs in new managers as well. This is the mind game we excel in. Once a manager believes they can achieve 100% occupancy, more likely than not, it will happen. That is the difference between good and great.

Chapter 5

Paying Attention to Details

There are certain things that make us unique in the industry. Let's face it, you don't have to be that good in order to achieve greatness in any given business. But what happens, especially in our business, is a lot of people miss the details. When we're looking at a property, our attention to detail is really where we stand out.

When I first started my apartment journey I was green and inexperienced. "*You don't know what you don't know.*" Let me share an example. We had a property with two old, faded and crooked stop signs located within the community boundaries. Half the time people drove right through them, not stopping or even appearing to notice the signs. When we brought in the management team we have now, they immediately said the stop signs really needed attention. One of them was tilting to the left and just looked haggard. That day, we dug those old, shabby signs out and replaced them. Now the property has brand new fresh, clean, straight stop signs. I never once thought about those signs before. I know the property staff and I had to have driven past them a million times. But we weren't focused on the details and, therefore, lost an opportunity to improve from good to great. That lesson was an invaluable one. From that moment on, I realized our success in managing properties lies in all the details inside the day-to-day operations. The by-product of our team putting up fresh new stop signs was immediate. Our tenants quickly noticed and began to make remarks when coming in to pay rent. "Nice stop signs." And "Man, you are really cleaning this place up" etc.

Who would have thought something as simple as a new stop sign would make that much of a difference? Yet it did and guess what? People actually stopped at them!

Why the Rich Get Richer

It's all about the details. It may seem inconsequential, but we pay attention to posts, the way they hang, the way they stand, what's on them. We look to see if the sign is faded or if it looks old or drab. We didn't pay attention to those things before, but now that's exactly what we do. We find those trivial things are what people tend to notice. They see them every day - when you replace them or freshen them up, it instills a sense of pride. Having tenants who are proud of their place of residence increases revenue. The apartment business is a mind game. We change our tenants' minds about the place they spend the most amount of their time. By making positive progress, you see a vibrant sense of community and pride. It doesn't happen overnight, but if we live and breathe it at the property level, it soon becomes fact.

Another element many operators do not place much value, as far as attention to detail, is the interior of a unit. We have purchased beautifully remodeled properties with new fixtures, tub surrounds, faucets and lighting. The previous owners felt they upgraded the property, and they certainly did. However, when we took a closer look at electrical outlet covers, faceplates on switches and sometimes even the switches themselves, we found them covered in dull, old paint. In our minds, how could they have come 95% of the way in remodeling a unit, preparing to turn it, yet not address the little details? Instead of investing an extra nominable amount of money, their final product rates, at best, 'handyman hacked'.

Forget doing a big remodel; what about just doing a fresh paint job? I've seen properties where people completed a brand-new paint job, but then reinstalled old, faded, and yellowish faceplates (circa 1970's). Again, most operators and management companies think that's okay. We don't understand why they didn't fully complete the project. Those faceplates and switches are so inexpensive, yet make all the difference. If we're going to redo a room and we're working on the electrical wiring, we're going to fix everything. You'd be surprised how many people have faceplates with four layers of paint. Why would they do that? You wouldn't want that in your house and people don't want that in their apartments.

Another example is door trim. I often see unmatched hinges and knobs. There could be gold hinges with a silver doorknob, and in other parts of the room there's a gold doorknob with silver hinges. The bottom line — the complex, and by extension, the property management company appears unprofessional. These insignificant items are such low-cost materials. It doesn't make sense why an owner wouldn't spend the money ensuring a smooth, cohesive, modern updated look. People pay attention. They may not notice when it's done right, but they will absolutely notice if it's done wrong.

The number of millennials and young adults who are moving into our apartments is rapidly increasing. This younger demographic is greatly connected to the information age and has different needs and hot

buttons than someone from the industrial age. Think about all of our device choices - cellphones, tablets, iPads, and iPods. The younger generation is heavily dependent and reliant upon these devices. Hotels are finally getting on board. We're beginning to see plug-in ports on nightstands and lamps. Most apartments don't have the plugin featuring a USB port. *see photo

Ours do. These typically only cost $10/each. Once again, they make a noticeable difference. We put them in the kitchen and bedrooms. Tenants have the ability to plug in cords, phones, pretty much anything that utilizes a USB - which is almost all devices. This is another reason we're ahead of our competition and is part of what makes us special - we address technology and anticipate tenant needs.

It's those minor things that always seem to mean a lot.

Our tenants are good hard-working people, and we want to treat them like the "A Tenant" they know and feel they are. This is called award-winning service. It's what keeps them at our property for years at a time. They don't want to leave because we're doing things to make them feel good and proud of where they live. Having happy tenants naturally evolves into quality referrals. This, in turn, equates to not having to spend marketing and advertising dollars to attract foot traffic to your property. You attract the exact type of tenant you currently have. This is the beautiful concept of duplication. Yet another way to increase profitability with little extra effort.

One of the biggest things we've gotten the most feedback from, especially from women, is our lighting package. Of everything we do to improve a property, this is our #1 bang for the buck. The results are immediate and improve the property overnight. We go in and remove the old, yellow, dingy incandescent energy burning lights and replace them with very high, bright white LED lights. Aesthetically, this makes an immediate world of a difference. Look at the image below to see the improvement.

On the first floor, we changed to LED lighting. The bright, white light feels clean, safe and attractive. The lighting in the second story looks dingy, yellow and murky. For many women, this equates to an unsafe environment.

Studies have shown women have a huge amount of influence in where a family lives. Do you think safety is a hot button for her? The answer is an absolute yes.

Why the Rich Get Richer

When a woman comes home at night and the lighting surrounding her apartment is like the second story pictured above, it will not sit well with her. On the other hand, when you show her pictures of the lighting changes you've made (with her safety in mind), you will win 99% of the time. I'm repeating here, but on purpose... one of the biggest bangs for our buck is our lighting. We make these improvements on every property we take on. Not only is the difference incredibly dramatic, but we receive immediate feedback from tenants. *Immediate.* They notice and appreciate our efforts and it helps us convey how and why Kahuna is different.

We don't stop with changing the lightbulbs. We go a step further and change interior breezeway light switches to automatic dawn-to-dusk timers. When darkness falls, these lights are set to come on and stay on. This ensures everything is bright. We do this for two reasons: the first is energy efficiency (not having lights on in daytime hours). Secondly, and more importantly, this prevents tenants (or others) from being able to turn off the light, the whole breezeway, or to utilize darkness as a shield to do anything undesirable. Terrible things usually happen in the dark, so by taking this step, we create a much safer area. When people understand the value of what this brings to an apartment community, it's priceless. Many questionable things could occur at night on property that a tenant is simply unaware of. Installing quality lighting in potentially suspect areas makes an enormous impact on the property.

The Checklist

For a unit to be ready for tenants, we have a "make ready" process. This technique is completed through management and systems, coupled with technology. Every time we do a "make ready" our maintenance person compiles a list of what's needed to make the unit ready for a new tenant. Remember, we normally know when someone is moving out. Since most tenants want to get their security deposit back, they happily work with our maintenance staff to gain entry and to review the unit. Upon the completion of all listed items, the maintenance person informs the Property Manager. He or she then comes in with a 30-point checklist. Similar to the pilot who flies a jumbo jet has a checklist, so do Kahuna Property Managers. Even though they've been through the same routine many times, they still utilize their list and check items off one by one. Implementing this into our system ensures even the little things, like taking the garbage out and cleaning appliances, are handled. These things matter. For example, how would you feel walking into a bathroom with old, dirty grout or black unsavory caulking in the corner? That's the death of a bathroom.

Upgrades

Traditionally, people were of the mindset that apartments needed to be white on white. White base, trim, and doors was the standard. People want something that feels more like a home. Class A properties normally have a two-tone paint palette. More or less, white paint and a nice warm colored paint cost the same. Why not add that nice earth-toned welcoming color? We make this upgrade in all Kahuna properties. We pay attention to color trends. Gray tones have been trending high, so we've transitioned into a hip light gray color with white trim. Whenever we are unsure on what to do for a property's color scheme, we simply visit a newly built Class A project. We use those color schemes and details as inspiration on what to incorporate into our property. It seems so basic, yet most people don't even think about it.

Thinking back to the little things we discussed, when a two-tone color palette is used, it really makes the room pop. The property stands out in comparison to others when it has color contrasting features. For us, two-tone paint is an absolute must.

We also replace and/or update ceiling fans. Many of the properties we purchase were built in the 1970's. Many times, they don't even have ceiling fans, or if they do the electrical wiring was installed incorrectly. We often see hanging cords that run from ceiling to ceiling to ceiling in little loops, in an attempt to get a power source up top for the fan to run.

It's easier and more efficient to install a dedicated electric line for a ceiling fan. A good electrician can do this job very cost-effectively. In master bedrooms, ceiling fans are a must. From a tenant's perspective, this means less money and energy spent on air conditioning. They can keep their home at a slightly higher temperature and use the fans to keep the unit cool. This naturally reduces their overall energy cost. We make sure to point that out to future residents.

Another example of a bang-for-the-buck-upgrade is microwaves. People will pay $20-$30 more per month to have a built-in microwave over the stove. It's certainly a nice feature. Microwaves are inexpensive nowadays. You can have one on the countertop, but it sure looks much nicer when it's above the stove

As far as flooring goes, the current trend is wood plank inspired vinyl. This gets installed in all major areas - living room, kitchen and hallways. Carpet lies in only the bedrooms. This is a big shift in the industry and for a good reason. It looks fantastic, and the vinyl lasts longer in these high traffic areas. Carpets would have to be replaced almost every year. Yet the vinyl will last several years, potentially allowing the turnover of a few tenants. By reducing carpet expenditures, we found another small area to increase profitability.

One of the last things we do is countertops and cabinets. Not surprisingly, these can be major ticket items. We find if the cabinets are generally in good shape, only the doors and hinges need replacing. In extreme cases, we have seen holes in the wood doors of a cabinet.

Usually it's very hard to find an exact match. When faced with this problem, a trick we often use is to find the closest match and install the new door. We then paint the entire cabinet either a dark coffee color, which is another current trend, or white. We save a great deal of money and also benefit from a fresh updated look without incurring the expense of cabinet replacement.

Regarding countertops, we've been using one particular trick for a while. Instead of replacing old linoleum counters we have found companies specializing in spackling. This spackle goes on the entire countertop and places a new sealant over it. It gives the countertop a fresh look and lasts several years. One mistake other operators make is replacing items rather than looking for ways to update and/or upgrade. They inevitably spend lots of Capital Improvement money that really could have been used elsewhere. Running efficiently is always key.

Wrapping it Up

To wrap up this chapter and put a bow on it, let's summarize what we are doing. When we buy a property, we look at how we can bring value with our cost sensitive upgrades. Every time we do these small upgrades, we call it "repositioning." We do them with the expectations of significantly increasing occupancy, or more importantly, increasing rent.

By bringing units up to a higher standard, and including items people want, it enables us to attract the very best tenant of any building classification. In other words, if we have a Class B property, our goal is to attract the best Class B tenants. These tenants also pay us the most (appropriate for location) rent. We are able to achieve this because these tenants want to stay at our property.

They always move to clean, affordable, perfectly maintained properties. This is the winning formula.

Why the Rich Get Richer

Very simply, our magic bullet is the detailed management piece no one seems to master like our company. It's really what separates us from others.

All these small savings and upgrades equate to being able to charge an additional $15 a month in rent. This, in turn, helps us attain a big yield. These small increases add up on a monthly basis and create a multiplying effect which is attractive to buyers when we sell the property. Income properties are based on net income. If you save $15 per unit, and increase rent by $15, that money shows up on the bottom line in the NOI, Net Operating Income. Let's take that effect on a 100-unit apartment complex and do the math.

Here's an easy example. Let's say we have that hundred-unit building and we can do some of these little things. First, the property buys an Industrial Carpet Cleaner for $500. By doing this, we no longer pay an outside vendor to clean carpets. This is roughly a savings of $60. But when applied to 100 units it quickly adds up, and significantly. Let's use the $15 savings per unit for this example. Next, we can easily increase the rent $15 per month. Most tenants consider this a nuisance increase and will not vacate for that amount of money. Now, we have increased our profits by $30 per door, per month. $30 times 100 doors equal $3,000. That, multiplied by 12 months in a year, equals $36,000. If we were to sell the property at a seven cap, we have now created an increase of $514,285 of value. We just made our property over half a million dollars more valuable by raising the rents and controlling costs.

Imagine that increase over the lifetime of a property. Most of our properties we buy and hold onto for five to ten years. If we're doing a $15 to $20 rent increase every year, what do you think that does to the value of our properties? It increases it substantially. You can easily get a $15 to $20 year after year rent increase. For $15 more a month in rent, most people are not going to complain, because it costs much more than that to move. In fact, all your competition is raising rents, too. So, if a tenant wanted to move, they would still have to pay rental increases. We just have to pay attention to the little things.

One last thing before I close. In the first year of a takeover, we complete upgrades and updates as quickly as possible. By doing this, our once vacant units get a substantial rent increase; sometimes up to $50 or $70, from the previously paid rent. This makes the value increase a lot.

However, we have bought properties where we have done very little and because we're buying from distressed owners, or owners that have deferred maintenance, or who are not seasoned operators, we find they're not operating at market value. In fact, many times they may be undervalued in their current rents by $15 or $20. This is another place we often find ourselves. We do very little and simply capitalize on another company not understanding their product and the market they were in. I very often find we can get the money other owners don't know about simply because they failed in operations and systems execution.

Chapter 6

Exterior Matters

The outside of the property is just as important, if not more so as the inside. After all, it's the first thing people see! First impressions matter!

Parking Areas

When we look at the exterior of a potential Kahuna property, one of the biggest detractors are the parking lots. This is a big-ticket item and most operators just look the other way. This improvement, however, brings your property back from the dead. When tenants see nice white lines marking parking spots and the pavement is jet black, it's a real eye catcher. By choosing to not upkeep pavement an owner will, over time, pay dearly as their parking lot becomes destroyed.

A low-cost item to fix quickly is the red NO PARKING zones or yellow Caution Zones along the curbing. Here, paint is your friend. A little elbow grease and some reflective paint is all that's required for those types of jobs and you are good to go. Can you say curb appeal?

Signage

We have discussed this, but one more time for good measure: your signage needs to look clean and up-to-date. If they look faded, they must go. Particularly the entry sign or marquis. This needs to stand out and be seen. It's the showpiece, after all. Often people think a property name change is necessary. We don't believe in that, but we will update signage to create a more attractive and enticing look.

Grounds

Often, when taking over a new property, the grounds are really overgrown. The shrubs are much bigger and much higher than they should be, and the trees aren't topped to look pretty or clean. By spending a week with your crew and having them cut all the unwanted overgrowth, it reveals your beautiful, well-maintained property. In the winter months, we do this to the extreme. We will cut all our bushes and shrubs way back and make massive tree topping happen. At first, our property looks naked and bare, but when spring finally arrives everything starts to fill in. It sure does make a difference.

We had a property with so many low-hanging tree limbs that many of them were almost hitting cars. Looking at the property from the street they were even obstructing views of the buildings. We trimmed the trees very, very high for a reason. Once completed, you could see the property again. It created an immediate visual effect. Simply trimming trees, bushes and shrubs, makes a powerful impact. Also, you can get a similar effect by planting shrubs and putting mulch where needed.

We do the grounds, trees, shrubs, and grass. Many times, Class B and C properties, depending on location, have grass but no sprinkler systems. Also, there's no chemical deterrent for weeds. The combination results in no grass, just a yard full of weeds.

Fortunately, when it's the right time of year, our team can grow grass from grass seeds. So, we look for property areas that need grass, and grow our own. It's not that hard. Many times, we'll start with a chemical company to treat the property first, killing all weeds. Then we fertilize at the proper time using the right amount to encourage grass to grow. This is not a quick process, usually taking a year or two to get the desired results. Because we do have a long-term outlook on our projects, the wait is always worth it. When you get a nice, full grassy area going that looks good, it makes a substantial difference on your property. That's what tenants are expecting, especially in "A" Properties.

It takes vision to understand these processes, as well as long term year after year execution. It's a vision we have both focused on and cultivated. We know who we are and what we value at the property level. Our philosophy allows the Kahuna team to see into the future, rather than simply looking for the overnight play opportunity. We're not doing fix and flip properties seen on TV. Our method is not the "try and make a quick buck" approach. We're operators, and there's a difference between the two. I think in this business there are guys who know how to do rehabs and they do it well. But when it comes to operations and running properties as a cash flow business with day-in and day-out operations, there are two distinctly separate ways to do that. There's a long-term vision, thinking about what's going on in the future and having a good idea or concept about it. Then there's the quick fix - fill it with anyone, hope to sell it, and make money. Our approach is always based on a cash flow model. What serves us well through both the good times and down is our consistency not only to our tenants, but our investors. When we're focused on service and providing quality affordable living, if and when people are looking for a residential change (due to economic factors) they'll strongly consider our options. We're doing all the unimportant Important things right, which improves operations.

Paint/Water Damage

On the actual structures, things like dinged-up downspouts, old screens, damaged fascia or peeling paint hurt the property. In addition to being an easy fix, paint is a protectant. It amazes me how many operators or owners of multi-million-dollar assets opt NOT to paint their buildings in order to keep water from destroying them. Water is your enemy and when left unchecked, it will destroy your buildings. Paint is your good friend. We paint almost every building we buy. It's simply a matter of replacing old wood fascia, or siding, then cleaning and repainting the whole project. Often, we see properties without drip-edge molding on the end of the roofs. This allows water to drip directly onto the fascia, leaving it ugly and looking unkempt. The owners leave it as is because they mistakenly believe that's the way it's supposed to look. We don't believe in that, so we'll replace the fascia. We'll install drip-edge molding so water leaves the building correctly and doesn't ruin our product.

You have a million dollars' worth of product, so why wouldn't you protect it with a hundred dollars of paint? It seems so simple! Yet, poor management leads to the unfortunate demise of a lot of properties. If you're not maintaining your paint, making sure everything is right and watertight, you are making a big mistake.

Downspouts/Gutters

Unattached downspouts look shabby and could be a potential problem and/or safety hazard. You want to ensure each downspout is securely fastened to the building. You also want to inspect the bottom to ensure grass or leaves have not gotten trapped, causing them to clog. This can cause problems.

If there are trees on your property, you should have a screen guard on top of the gutters. This will keep them from clogging and sagging. Unless you want to climb a ladder two or three times a season, it's a wise idea to invest in these leaf guards. Replacing gutters is not very expensive, but a beaten-up gutter or downspout is sure to draw attention. When the water comes out, right at the end of the guttering, we have concrete diverters. Not having these creates an unsightly bare spot where grass will not grow due to water erosion. Why not attach a device that will move rainwater out where it dispenses a little further, less violently? Again, attention to the little things.

Siding

If there are areas where siding is broken, fix it. For faded segments, use a specialized product you paint directly onto the vinyl designed to extend the life of the siding. You can even remove a piece of the siding from the back of the building and use it on your front patches. Then install the new pieces where they're less visible or put all the new pieces on one building.

Pets

We do allow pets at our properties. However, we have size and weight restrictions. If a property allows pets, it's only necessary and natural to have "poop stations". If there are enough stations on site, people will use them. Then it's management's responsibility to monitor. Nothing works without monitoring. The community needs to take accountability If they think the maintenance staff is going to remove the poop, then they will make no effort to clean up after their pet(s). We're either training them or they're training us.

This means we're watching. Let's say it's early morning, a tenant allows his/her dogs to relieve themselves yet the tenant ignores the mess. We'll have someone pick up the mess, but also officially cite the tenant. That gets their attention quickly and word spreads. More than likely, everybody starts using the poop stations. They know it's unacceptable to ignore it, they take responsibility, and the poop gets picked up. It's amazing, but little things like those poop stations work.

Common Areas

Proper management and maintenance makes a dramatic difference. Carry the same approach over into the public areas - laundry area, community and mailbox areas. Make sure you have trash bins at the mailboxes. People want to throw junk mail away, so make it convenient for your tenants by placing a trash can nearby.

We also try to make communal recreational areas. Not every community can accommodate them but when possible, we like to have a space for tenants to get together and cookout or barbecue. We've added benches with some type of a gazebo, or another structure that offers sun protection. Fire pits are also popular. These elements are always nice added touches. More importantly, they create a wonderful community atmosphere and environment.

A great deal of our tenants have families, so playgrounds are another big selling point. It's only natural to expect children to be in a two- or three-bedroom unit. Our playgrounds may not feature the newest equipment, but we have them, nonetheless. There's always a barrier or fence of some sort around the area. Additionally, we use soft rubber mulch that will protect the kids and keep the playground safe and clean. We try to anticipate and address every issue we can when preparing our properties.

Playgrounds are a big feature to a property. It's essential to keep the area clean, and therefore our maintenance staff inspects the playground daily. We look for vandalism and anything else that requires attention. Our team repairs and corrects any issues to ensure the equipment looks sharp.

Security Cameras

We believe security is of the utmost importance at all Kahuna properties. We like to embrace all available technology. Video monitoring is affordable enough that we can mount wireless cameras on our buildings. We are usually able to locate a power source in the buildings. This allows us to install cameras all over the property. The impact is felt again, immediately. We purchase and install a 52" TV monitor behind our Leasing Manager's desk. The live video streams from the security cameras are constantly playing on those monitors. Anyone applying for a lease can see we have security measures in place. People take notice. Cameras help deter undesirable activity.

With women and safety in mind, yet again, our properties typically have some type of surveillance system. It makes a big difference and dramatically reduces crime.

Swimming Pools

Almost every apartment or multi-family complex has a pool. The first thing anybody looks at is pool water quality. Does it look clean or is it foggy? Our maintenance staff is trained to handle the pool and if there's ever a major problem we call a pool professional right away. What people don't realize is, keeping a pool crystal clear is important, but you also have an area where you can style and showcase your property.

You want to try and make your pool area an oasis. This can be achieved by simply adding large pots with flowers or with small little trees in pots. It's a beautiful place to put tables with colorful umbrellas. Bring vibrant color into the area to make it nice, warm and inviting. We have even purchased chaise lounge covers. The plastic lounges are inexpensive, but that doesn't mean we shouldn't protect and preserve them. Most home improvement stores will carry inexpensive, yet decent quality lounge chair covers. This again makes the pool area colorful and vibrant. Know that covers sometimes only last about a year, so with replacement in mind, look for inexpensive.

By doing this simple thing, every year our chaise covers look awesome and bring color and vibrancy to our pool area. That sells. Even though in some places the pool may only be open for three or four months, tenants love it. They love pool time.

Shade is also important. Typically, we have three or four areas with umbrellas where people can sit down and visit. A lot of operators underestimate the value of the pool. And even though the pool is not always used, it's always noted. It really makes a difference to have a nice pool area. We want it to be memorable and a place to have fun.

Chapter 7

Extracurricular Activities

We are only a chapter away from being done, and I want to take this time to go over some other important things about me and what I've been able to achieve. More importantly, I want to express my sincere gratitude that you have made it this far.

In my life, I have had points in time where things I did changed me dramatically. I often think back to those times and feel blessed for taking action. I've spent six chapters explaining to you how I've mastered the apartment process. I did that not on my own, but by empowering a team. I used to be the guy who was a jack of all trades but really a master of none. Once I figured out I need only master one, my income and knowledge grew.

I also have come to understand that my gift is raising Private Capital and team building. In those two areas, I have excelled. I learned early on that by putting myself in leadership positions, it helped open more and more opportunities to share my story and help others at the same time.

For example, I've taught how to open a business, create a product and put it up for sale using the Junior Achievement Platform at high schools. This work is truly enjoyable. By doing what I love, it has allowed me to meet other successful businessmen and women over the years that enjoy the same thing. Because we had a common bond, we eventually learned more about each other and our businesses. It should be no surprise that many of my investors come from the Junior Achievement program. The goal is never to join a group or become involved in a cause simply because there may be something in it for you. Do so to find things you value, like to do and to meet people - despite yourself. It's just what happens. Better yet, you will also find that doing business with other services is very rewarding. It's just better to do business with people you like.

We are nearing the end, and you should now have a pretty good understanding of who I am and what I stand for. You may be asking yourself questions like, "How's my financial portfolio treating me lately?" Or "Do I understand what my investments are in?" Or my favorite, "Is my portfolio actually diversified?" When people invest with us, they become actual shareholders on the LLC that owns an apartment building. Our investors receive a K-1 each year on the income they have made, minus depreciation. Wait, I just mentioned "depreciation" and we have not talked about it yet! Depreciation is the term for what you can write off from a building purchase, minus the value of land. Once you get that amount, you then divide that amount by 27.5, which is the rate allowed for multi-family buildings. So, if we bought a $4.5 million property and the land was worth $1 million, we would now take $3.5 million and divide by 27.5. That equals $127,272 of depreciation that the property will share with all investors in the deal. Pretty awesome, right?

If you want to know more on how you can get your money working a little harder for you go to **www.WhyTheRichGetRicher.net/income**. I want to give you my Credibility Kit and create an opportunity to discuss your income goals and dreams.

It's a Good Problem to Have

You see, I have a problem. We have become so successful at locating excellent cash flowing apartment deals. These deals are of course where we implement all the strategies covered in this book. And therein lies my problem. We now have more deals than we have private money with which to invest. That is, in part, my reason for writing this book. We have helped so many investors realize both their income goals with "mailbox money" and their overall growth goals. We accomplish this simply by using the multi-family class of assets and of course, being top-of-the-line operators. I know there are more people looking for what Kahuna Investments has to offer. I have a problem, but if you're reading this book, chances are you're the solution.

We have grown operationally to a point where we can feed a consistent growth pattern and not disrupt our attention to detail. Now it's about sourcing the capital to simply have an opportunity to grow.

When investors first meet me, and see the concepts on paper, they are very cautious. This is a quality trait. But as we dive deeper and validate the process using actuals and financial reporting, most investors come away with the attitude of "let's give it a try." What that means is no one upon the first meeting says, "Corey, I've got $1.2 million to invest and I want to give it all to Kahuna." That has never happened and I doubt it ever will. Instead, a lot of people come into their first deal with $100K to test the waters. They want to evaluate our execution of our strategies and, bottom line, for my company to deliver. Usually when the second quarterly cash flow check comes in, our partners are hooked. Then they opt to "go bigger" - sometimes sharing with us the $500K to $1 million in funds they would like to place in the next deal. Currently, our number one source of new investors is referrals.

When you treat people right, word gets around.

Our structured business model for apartment investing helps two core groups of individuals. The first core group we work with is made up of retirees looking for income streams. Our investment works well for this type of investor because the apartments earn monthly rental income. We then take those profits and pay quarterly income to the partnership. We average between a 4-7% preferred return. This means if you invested $100,000 each year you would get between $4,000-$7,000 annually or $1,000-$1,750 quarterly. That is considered a solid return for most.

BUT WAIT, THERE'S MORE....

Remember, we hold for cash flow and then eventually sell the apartment complex. This enables us to provide an additional return to our investors. On average, we aim for an additional 5-7% return (per year held) upon the sale of the property. Both returns combined - cash flow and profit from the sale, yield between 9%-14%.

Because we can achieve this kind of return, it attracts the second core investor group. This investor is looking for overall growth. Because we base our deals on cash flow, these investors see our deals as a solid way to earn consistent return year after year... without having years of loss.

The Kicker

We always strictly follow all SEC rules and guidelines. We wouldn't have been able to, in good conscience, publish this book otherwise. Anyone coming to us from this publication can only participate in our deals if they are an accredited investor. An investor is accredited by meeting one of two requirements: annual income of at least $250,000 (single) or $350,000 (couple); or net worth of $1,000,000 (excluding primary residence). These accreditations are non-negotiable and will be properly and appropriately verified. Our investments also have risk – we never enter a deal in anticipation of a loss, but the risk is there nonetheless. Taking on a questionable investor is simply not prudent business practice.

The process of how we sell our properties for maximum profit will be detailed in the next chapter, but let's start with a general strategy overview.

Why the Rich Get Richer

Our typical hold time on most properties is five years. There's a reason for that. Our loans normally go five years before the yield maintenance fee is only 1%. This is the fee you must pay the bank if you leave early. Typically, year one is 5% and then it goes down a percent every year. Currently, while writing this, we are doing a 7-year fixed loan that has a 13-year adjustable rate after the first seven. This loan has a 1% fee at the end of five years. We added the 13-year adjustable loan for insurance.

What do I mean by "insurance?" At some point in the future, our market will inevitably go down. The problem is no one knows when. After living through the recession in 2008-2009, I learned several things. Many investors in the apartment world had five-year contracts (very typical in the industry). When the market crashed, many of these properties were operating fine on a cash flow model. Many properties had loans coming due in 2008 and 2009. Normally, that's not a big deal. But in the Great Recession, it didn't matter that the property cash flowed. The problem was that banks were not granting loans. Many cash flowing assets were foreclosed on because they could not source equitable debt. This is our main driver and what we call insurance. If the market takes a downturn and banks will not lend with reasonable rates, I want a loan that can extend out farther in term.

Once we reach the five-year mark, we look at exit strategies. Many times, we refinance with a new loan and cash out all investors. We use a certified appraisal and use their figure as our sale price. We then figure our numbers to calculate profit and distribute proceeds as provided in the PPM Guidelines.

Other times, we will just sell the asset on the open market. We have a unique way of doing this, which we explain in detail in the next chapter. This does help to create a lot of value.

With a lot of value comes taxes. I'm not sure about you, but taxes are something I try to avoid at all cost. When we sell an asset, we normally look to do a 1031 exchange. This means if we find another property, we use all profits from the first sale to move onto the next deal. This works great, but only works if each investor is on board.

So, here's your last chance to take action!

Go to **www.WhyTheRichGetRicher.net/income** to get my Credibility Kit and let's start a conversation on how my company can potentially help you.

Most wealthy people I know work incredibly hard in their chosen profession. It's fairly common knowledge that real estate should be part of one's investment portfolio. However, most do not have the capacity to carve out the 1,000's of hours needed to become a real estate Wudan Sholin Monk Master. The good news is I have already put in the time, and I want to help you.

We're looking to bring in a new group of investors to continue our growth and continue efforts to make a difference in the communities we serve.

Chapter 8

Selling Your Property

When it's time to sell the property, at this level you're always going to use a realtor, a commercial broker. As we ready to list a property, we do a couple things considered opposite of the norm. First and foremost, we share part of the profit with our management company. Why would I do that, you may be asking? There are two reasons. First, if the management company is financially "tied" to goal realization – to deliver as much NOI as possible to our P&L - they are highly motivated. This means the entire team is on board. Secondly, by doing number one, it allows me to focus on what I do best - team building and raising capital. I'm not focused on or consumed with daily property operations. I have trained professionals incentivized for us all to do well. It perfectly aligns our common goals.

This creates a ripple effect - the management team shares the money they've made with all on and off-site staff. This creates an open and honest working environment. When we're ready to sell a property, it's announced within our entire system. It is to be celebrated and honored. I can't tell you how many times I've encountered the opposing scenario – secrets, requests to not visit properties, etc. This is usually very awkward and not conducive to my goal when on-site - to gather as much info as possible. Sharing this information with the team and letting them know they have bonuses on the way, creates a wonderful culture. This is directly related to why the management team usually stays at the property with the next owner as well. It happens quite frequently with us. By doing this one simple thing, we now have motivated employees selling our property to potential buyers. That is a wow factor. Who better to sell the property than the people with boots on the ground? We train them on this process and is another KPI.

The next unique thing we do is we only use our preferred broker to sell all our apartments. Freddy Spencer with Century 21 in Columbia, Missouri is amazing. Freddy understands our process and is used to our crazy recommendations. When we sell a property, our most important goal is to never be motivated. We are very happily unmotivated to sell. Because of this, we list our property at a very high price and an extremely low cap rate. It's like fishing...everyone wants to catch a fish, but not many understand how to catch the big bass. To catch a bass, you must be in the right spot at the right time with the right bait. In the apartment world, this equates to monthly financials (for last five years) detailing our methodical growth progress. We have taken care of the property and maintained it to a very high degree and have not deferred maintenance; the right place. Because we have almost 100% ACH adoption from our tenants, we have consistent turn-key collections. We create an environment where all you have to do is come in and enjoy the ride. We've got the right bait.

We set our bait, the perfect apartment model, and wait for the big bass - Family Office Fund money or dissolved 1031 exchanges needing to quickly identify an asset to close. Our intention is to create solid cash flowing solutions for the "big guys" so they will buy property at crazy cap rates.

Why does this happen? Why would people pay so much? Because we solve problems and we understand marketing. We market to the very individuals listed above and share our solutions. More importantly, we believe we can. The power of our minds should never be underestimated. It's called posture. You usually find what you look for, and in this case, we look to sell our properties for a lot of money. Often, we find what we are looking for.

Now let's move more into the operations of getting a property ready.

This is not a one-man show and by now you are aware the entire team plays an important role.

Maintenance

From a maintenance perspective, we ensure our grounds are immaculate. We know the importance of appearance. We make sure everything is on point - mulch, trim, any place we see needing attention. If work is needed, we submit a work order to confirm it will be addressed. With a minimum of five years showing solid financials, our properties command a premium. Our books are completed to the highest of standards. I've learned when you have solid financials, backed by a well-kept property, you'll attract the best deal.

Financials

We operate efficiently not only in our day-to-day interactions at the property level, but with our financial process as well. We have open, clean, and full detailed accounting for our properties. In other words, we have nothing to hide. This allows us to show a very solid, consistent, predictable income when looking over yearly performance. If someone were to take a detailed look at our P&L's, they would see steady income growth trends coupled with tight control of expenses. We often can sell at a cap rate other people don't understand, yet question. There have been many instances where we bought property at an eight cap and sold it at a five cap. The reason for this is, we are never motivated sellers. We put our properties up for sale knowing that if they don't sell, we are perfectly fine. This mindset allows us to target and market to an investor group that fits in two categories. One target buyer is a buying group that may be coming out of a broker 1031 exchange. This means the group sold a property and had a great deal of time to both identify and buy a new one. This allowed them to avoid paying taxes on their earned profits. They would rather buy a solid performing cash flowing property than suffer a large tax hit. The second buyer we target is what I call East and West Coast Family Office money. These groups are not yield driven. Instead, they are looking for steady income with predictability. When these groups investigate or check into our books, they see these trends - which equal big money.

We showed this example in the beginning of the book, but it's powerful and worth sharing again. Let's say there is $100,000 of NOI (Net Operating Income) for a property, at an eight cap, worth $1,250,000. If I take the same $100,000 of NOI, and divide it by a six cap, it's $1,666,000 – a difference of roughly $400,000. This is a huge increase in value. Keep in mind, we're only using an example of $100,000 NOI. However, our properties are usually setting off $400,000 of NOI. When you take the same amount, and multiply it times four, it's significant. The cap rate makes a dramatic difference in the value of your property.

Because the cap rate is important, ensuring our product is perfect is of the utmost importance. It pays off when we get an offer and close. Just as there is a process for buying a property, we have one for selling as well. When a potential buyer sends us an LOI we then find ourselves on the other end of the transaction. When we get an offer, most likely the buying group fits our metrics, as we have artificially priced our property very high. We simply negotiate the timing, deposits and close of escrow to agreeable terms and then start the selling process. It's important for our team at this point to be functioning well and in tune. It takes 90-120 days to close a property. During the sales process, we must maintain our operational performance. Luckily for us, because we use the incentive program and share in the profits of the sale, everyone on our team is on point. Which leads to the close of escrow.

When we close, it's a pretty cool feeling. The team enjoys a kind of little happy dance. It's important to take time to celebrate a success. It feels good when you sell a big property knowing the team all had a part in the process. In addition, it never hurts when you make a lot of money.

Private Placement

From an accounting standpoint, we must have all proper documentation. It's non-negotiable when raising millions of dollars of other people's money. We always incorporate a Private Placement Memorandum, or PPM. Whenever you pull more than one person's money into an investment, you are creating a security. And our government regulates this through the Securities and Exchange Commissions, or SEC. A PPM is a document created by a legal professional trained in the SEC Law. Its purpose is to dictate how to pool money for an investment. It also details the process for paying investors, as well as explains the potential risk that could wipe out or cause you to lose the Investment. Our Private Placements are deal specific, meaning we raise capital for one particular project.

The SEC regulates a PPM, and for this reason, they are taken very seriously. The PPM dictates how you operate and we follow this blueprint to its exact instructions. You can pay an attorney $15,000 to $25,000 to properly construct the documents for private placement, so it's not cheap. We don't take it lightly and we follow our instructions. Setting up our documents correctly allows our investors peace of mind. This creates credibility and trust that we are not a "fly-by-night operation." We have high integrity in our business practice.

What happens when we sell a property and the escrow company disburses the profits into our main operating account? That's a common question I get from many investors. Our answer is straight forward. We don't immediately disburse funds. This is due to the fact there are often remaining expenses that still need to be paid. There may be a water or electric bill yet to come. Utility companies typically bill for services right up to our closing date. The amount, considered the property's expenses, can often be $20,000 - $25,000. We hold the money and wait another 30 days. This allows any remaining bills to cycle through. Once we have all bills accounted for, we then split profits based upon the PPM waterfall.

Now What?

At this point in our investors' experience, they have been with us about five years. They have not only received quarterly payments for five straight years, but they just received a chunk of money when we sold the property. This is the reason we have between a 70% to 80% retention rate. Our investors like the income stream; they like the payoff at the end. They like the complete process for the same reason the people to whom we sell our properties like it. Predictable income is sexy... Our investors want predictable income in their investments and that's what we provide.

Implementing what we know best, we employ investor capital for multi-family investing. Our technology and systems allow us to provide investors with predictable income. I get to live my dream doing the deals I love, making money for my investors. When my investors make money, it means I'm making money, too. It's a good business model and we enjoy great partnerships. Some of those relationships become lifelong relationships and it's a lot of fun.

Conclusion

I had no idea what I was going to be when I grew up. It took me a while to get the message, the "download" if you will, from the mothership as to what I was supposed to do with my life. There aren't many who can honestly say they do what they love. All I can tell you, my friends, is I truly love playing Monopoly. I love the real estate game. Not only have I enjoyed the countless hours spent mastering my craft, I have enjoyed the journey even more. The growth I have realized has helped all aspects of my life. I give more, I feel more, I love more, and I pray more. The more I moved away from "what's in it for me" and moved into "how can I help others", the more my business has grown. Helping others achieve their financial goals is a rewarding experience. Helping others, period, can do more for you than you think. This is why I now enjoy teaching others.

It's humbling to think about where I started, compared to where I am now. Never did I dream of this much success. I, of course, did not do this alone. I have so many people to thank for this journey. Through this process, I learned a lot about myself and who I am. I made a promise to myself that I would never get lost in the real estate game. I made a promise to myself that I would never let the pursuit of money and things be the driving force in my life. Most importantly, I promised to always remain myself. I would always be the kid who dreamed big, who had a big heart, who loved others and who knew if he just put his mind to something, he could achieve anything. I feel I have achieved that in writing this book. My hope is, not only have you learned something, but you have enjoyed reading it as well.

Why the Rich Get Richer

Glossary

Real estate investors will find this glossary helpful in understanding words and terms used in real estate transactions. However, some factors may affect these definitions. Terms are defined as they are commonly understood in the mortgage and real estate industry. The same terms may have different meanings in another context. The definitions are intentionally general, nontechnical, and short. They do not encompass all possible meanings or nuances that a term may acquire in legal use. State laws, as well as custom and use in various states or regions of the country, may in fact modify or completely change the meanings of certain defined terms. Before signing any documents or depositing any money preparatory to entering into a real estate contract, the purchaser should consult with an attorney to ensure that his or her rights are properly protected.

Abstract of Title: A summary of the public records relating to the title to a particular piece of land. An attorney or title insurance company reviews an abstract of title to determine whether there are any title defects that must be cleared before a buyer can purchase clear, marketable, and insurable title.

Acceleration Clause: Condition in a mortgage that may require the balance of the loan to become due immediately in the event regular mortgage payments are not made or for breach of other conditions of the mortgage.

Ad Valorem: Designates an assessment of taxes against property in a literal sense according to its value.

Adjustable Rate Mortgage Loans (ARM): Loans with interest rates that are adjusted periodically based on changes in a preselected index. As a result, the interest rate on your loan and the monthly payment will rise and fall with increases and decreases in overall interest rates. These mortgage loans must specify how their interest rate changes, usually in terms of a relation to a national index such as (but not always) Treasury bill rates. If interest rates rise, your monthly payments will rise. An interest rate cap limits the amount by which the interest rate can change; look for this feature when you consider an ARM loan.

Adverse Possession: A possession that is inconsistent with the right of possession and title of the true owner. It is the actual, open, notorious, exclusive, continuous, and hostile occupation and possession of the land of another under a claim of right or under color of title.

Agency: The relationship that exists by contract whereby one-person is authorized to represent and act on behalf of another person in various business transactions.

Agreement of Sale: Known by various names, such as contract of purchase, purchase agreement, or sales agreement, according to location or jurisdiction. A contract in which a seller agrees to sell and a buyer agrees to buy, under certain specific terms and conditions spelled out in writing and signed by both parties.

Amortization: A payment plan that enables the borrower to reduce a debt gradually through monthly payments of principal, thereby liquidating or extinguishing the obligation through a series of installments.

Annual Compounding: The arithmetic process of determining the final value of a cash flow or series of cash flows when interest is added once a year.

Annual Percentage Rate (APR): The cost of credit expressed as a yearly rate. The annual percentage rate is often not the same as the interest rate. It is a percentage that results from an equation considering the amount financed, the finance charges, and the term of the loan.

Appraisal: An expert judgment or estimate of the quality or value of real estate as of a given date. The process through which conclusions of property value are obtained. It is also referring to the formalized report that sets forth the estimate and conclusion of value.

Appurtenance. That which belongs to something else. In real estate law, an appurtenance is a right, privilege, or improvement, which passes as an incident to the land, such as a right of way.

Assessed Value: An official valuation of property most often used for tax purposes.

Assignment: The method or manner by which a right, a specialty, or contract is transferred from one person to another.

Assumption of Mortgage: An obligation undertaken by the purchaser of property to be personally liable for payment of an existing mortgage. In an assumption, the purchaser is substituted for the original mortgagor in the mortgage instrument and the original mortgagor is to be released from further liability in the assumption. The mortgagee's consent is usually required.

The original mortgagor should always obtain a written release from further liability to be fully released under the assumption. Failure to obtain such a release renders the original mortgagor liable if the person assuming the mortgage fails to make the monthly payments.

An assumption of mortgage is often confused with 'purchasing subject to a mortgage.' When one purchases subject to a mortgage, the purchaser agrees to make the monthly mortgage payments on an existing mortgage, but the original mortgagor remains personally liable if the purchaser fails to make the monthly payments. Since the original mortgagor remains liable in the event of default, the mortgagee's consent is not required for a sale subject to a mortgage.

Both assumption of mortgage and purchasing subject to a mortgage are used to finance the sale of property. They may also be used when a mortgagor is in financial difficulty and desires to sell the property to avoid foreclosure.

Balance Statement: A statement of the firm's financial position at a specific point in time.

Balloon Mortgage: Balloon mortgage loans are short-term fixed-rate loans with fixed monthly payments for a set number of years followed by one large final balloon payment ("the balloon") for the remainder of the principal. Typically, the balloon payment may be due at the end of 5, 7, or 10 years. Borrowers with balloon loans may have the right to refinance the loan when the balloon payment is due, but the right to refinance is not guaranteed.

Bankruptcy: A proceeding in a federal court to relieve certain debts of a person or a business unable to pay its debts.

Bill of Sale: A written document or instrument that provides evidence of the transfer of right, title, and interest in personal property from one person to another.

Binder or Offer to Purchase: A preliminary agreement, secured by the payment of earnest money, between a buyer and seller as an offer to purchase real estate. A binder secures the right to purchase real estate upon agreed terms for a limited period of time. If the buyer decides not to purchase/is unable to purchase, the earnest money is forfeited unless the binder expressly provides that it is to be refunded.

Blanket Mortgage: A single mortgage that covers more than one piece of real estate. It is often used to purchase a large tract of land, which is later subdivided and sold as individual parcels.

Bona fide: Made in good faith; good, valid, without fraud; such as a *bona fide* offer.

Bond: Any obligation under seal. A real estate bond is a written obligation, usually issued on security of a mortgage or deed of trust.

Breach: The breaking of law, or failure of a duty, either by omission or commission; the failure to perform, without legal excuse, any promise that forms a part or the whole of a contract.

Broker: One who is engaged for others in a negotiation for contacts relative to property, with the custody of which they have no concern.

Broker, Real Estate: Any person, partnership, association, or corporation who, for a compensation or valuable consideration, sells or offers for sale, buys or offers to buy, or negotiates the purchase or sale or exchange of real estate, or rents or offers to rent, any real estate or the improvements thereon for others.

Capital: Accumulated wealth; a portion of wealth set aside for the production of additional wealth; specifically, the funds belonging to the partners or shareholders of a business, invested with the express purpose and intent of remaining in the business to generate profits.

Capital Expenditures: Investments of cash or other property, or the creation of a liability in exchange for property to remain permanently in the business; usually pertaining to land, buildings, machinery, and equipment.

Capitalization: The act or process of converting or obtaining the present value of future incomes into current equivalent capital value; also, the amount so determined; commonly referring to the capital structure of a corporation or other such legal entity.

Cash Out: Any cash received when a new loan is obtained that is larger than the remaining balance of the current mortgage, based upon the equity already built up in the property. The cash-out amount is calculated by subtracting the sum of the old loan and fees from the new mortgage loan.

Caveat Emptor: The phrase literally means "let the buyer beware." Under this doctrine, the buyer is duty bound to examine the property being purchased and assumes conditions that are readily ascertainable upon view.

Certificate of Title: A certificate issued by a title company or a written opinion rendered by an attorney that the seller has good marketable and insurable title to the property offered for sale. A certificate of title offers no protection against any hidden defects in the title that an examination of the records could not reveal. The issuer of a certificate of title is liable only for damages due to negligence. The protection offered a homeowner under a certificate of title is not as great as that offered in a title insurance policy.

Chain of Title: A history of conveyances and encumbrances affecting the title to a particular real property.

Chattel: Items of moveable personal property, such as animals, household furnishings, money, jewelry, motor vehicles, and all other items not permanently affixed to real property that can be transferred from one place to another.

Closing Costs: The numerous expenses that buyers and sellers normally incur to complete a transaction in the transfer of ownership of real estate. These costs are in addition to price of the property and are items prepaid at the closing day. The following is a common list of closing costs.

BUYER'S EXPENSES:

- ✓ Documentary Stamps on Notes
- ✓ Recording Deed and Mortgage
- ✓ Escrow Fees
- ✓ Attorney's Fee
- ✓ Title Insurance
- ✓ Appraisal and Inspection
- ✓ Survey Charge

SELLER'S EXPENSES:

- ✓ Cost of Abstract
- ✓ Documentary Stamps on Deed
- ✓ Real Estate Commission
- ✓ Recording Mortgage
- ✓ Survey Charge
- ✓ Escrow Fees
- ✓ Attorney's Fee

The agreement of sale negotiated previously between the buyer and the seller may state in writing who will pay each of the above costs.

Closing Day: The day on which the formalities of a real estate sale are concluded. The certificate of title, abstract, and deed are generally prepared for the closing by an attorney and this cost is charged to the buyer. The buyer signs the mortgage, and closing costs are paid. The final closing merely confirms the original agreement reached in the agreement of sale.

Cloud on Title: An outstanding claim or encumbrance that adversely affects the marketability of title.

Collateral Security: A separate obligation attached to a contract to guarantee its performance; the transfer of property or of other contracts or valuables to ensure the performance of a principal agreement or obligation.

Commission: Money paid to a real estate agent or broker by the seller as compensation for finding a buyer and completing the sale. Usually it is a percentage of the sale price ranging anywhere from 6 to 7 percent on single-family houses and 10 percent on land.

Compound Interest: Interest paid on the original principal of an indebtedness and also on the accrued and unpaid interest that has accumulated over time.

Condominium: Individual ownership of a dwelling unit and an individual interest in the common areas and facilities serving the multi-unit project.

Consideration: Something of value, usually money, that is the inducement of a contract. Any right, interest, property, or benefit accruing to one party; any forbearance, detriment, loss or responsibility given, suffered or undertaken, may constitute a consideration that will sustain a contract.

Contract of Purchase: (*See* agreement of sale)

Conventional Mortgage: A mortgage loan not insured by HUD or guaranteed by the Veterans' Administration. It is subject to conditions established by the lending institution and state statutes. The mortgage rates may vary with different institutions and between states. (States have various interest limits.)

Cooperative Housing: An apartment building or a group of dwellings owned by a corporation, the stockholders of which are the residents of the dwellings. It is operated for their benefit by their elected board of directors. In a cooperative, the corporation or association owns title to the real estate. A resident purchases stock in the corporation, which entitles the resident to occupy a unit in the building or property owned by the cooperative. While the resident does not own the unit, the resident has an absolute right to occupy that unit for as long as he or she owns the stock.

Covenant: An agreement between two or more persons entered into by deed whereby one of the parties promises the performance of certain acts, or that a given state does or shall, or does not or shall not, exist.

Debt: An obligation to repay a specified amount at a specified time.

Debt Service: The portion of funds required to repay a financial obligation such as a mortgage, which includes interest and principal payments.

Deed: A formal written instrument by which title to real property is transferred from one owner to another. The deed should contain an accurate description of the property being conveyed, should be signed and witnessed according to the laws of the state where the property is located, and should be delivered to the purchaser on the day of closing. There are two parties to a deed—the grantor and the grantee. (*See also* deed of trust, general warranty deed, quitclaim deed, and special warranty deed.)

Deed of Trust: Just like a mortgage, a security instrument whereby real property is given as security for a debt; however, in a deed of trust there are three parties to the instrument—the borrower, the trustee, and the lender (or beneficiary). In such a transaction, the borrower transfers the legal title for the property to the trustee, who holds the property in trust as security for the payment of the debt to the lender or beneficiary. If the borrower pays the debt as agreed, the deed of trust becomes void. If, however, the borrower defaults in the payment of the debt, the trustee may sell the property at a public sale, under the terms of the deed of trust. In most jurisdictions where the deed of trust is in force, the borrower is subject to having the property sold without benefit of legal proceedings. A few states have begun in recent years to treat the deed of trust like a mortgage.

Default: Failure to make mortgage payments as agreed to in a commitment based on the terms and at the designated time set forth in the mortgage or deed of trust. It is the mortgagor's responsibility to remember the due date and send the payment prior to the due date, not after. Generally, 30 days after the due date if payment is not received, the mortgage is in default. In the event of default, the mortgagor may give the lender the right to accelerate payments, take possession and receive rents, and start foreclosure. Defaults may also come about by the failure to observe other conditions in the mortgage or deed of trust.

Depreciation: Decline in value of a house due to wear and tear, adverse changes in the neighborhood, or any other reason. The term is most often applied for tax purposes.

Down Payment: The amount of money to be paid by the purchaser to the seller upon the signing of the agreement of sale. The agreement of sale will refer to the down payment amount and will acknowledge receipt of the down payment. Down payment is the difference between the sales price and maximum mortgage amount. The down payment may not be refundable if the purchaser fails to buy the property without good cause. If the purchaser wants the down payment to be refundable, a clause in the agreement of sale should be inserted, specifying the conditions under which the deposit will be refunded, if the agreement does not already contain such clause. If the seller cannot deliver good title, the agreement of sale usually requires the seller to return the down payment and to pay interest and expenses incurred by the purchaser.

Duress: Unlawful constraint exercised upon a person, whereby the person is forced to perform some act, or to sign an instrument or document against his or her will.

Earnest Money: The deposit money given to the seller or the seller's agent by the potential buyer upon the signing of the agreement of sale to show serious intent about buying a house or any other type of real property. If the sale goes through, the earnest money is applied against the down payment. If the sale does not go through, the earnest money will be forfeited or lost unless the binder or offer to purchase expressly provides that it is refundable.

Easement Rights: A right-of-way granted to a person or company authorizing access to or over the owner's land. An electric company obtaining a right-of-way across private property is a common example.

Economic Life: The period over which a property may be profitably utilized or the period over which a property will yield a return on the investment, over and above the economic or ground rent due to its land.

Economic Obsolescence: Impairment of desirability or useful life arising from economic forces, such as changes in optimum land use, legislative enactments that restrict or impair property rights, and changes in supply and demand relationships.

Eminent Domain: The superior right of property subsisting in each and every sovereign state to take private property for public use upon the payment of just compensation. This power is often conferred upon public service corporations that perform quasi-public functions, such as providing public utilities. In every case, the owner whose property is taken must be justly compensated according to fair market values in the prevailing area.

Encroachment: An obstruction, building, or part of a building that intrudes beyond a legal boundary onto neighboring private or public land, or a building extending beyond the building line.

Encumbrance: A legal right or interest in land that affects a good or clear title and diminishes the land's value. It can take numerous forms, such as zoning ordinances, easement rights, claims, mortgages, liens, charges, a pending legal action, unpaid taxes, or restrictive covenants. An encumbrance does not legally prevent transfer of the property to another. A title search is all that is usually done to reveal the existence of such encumbrances, and it is up to the buyer to determine whether to purchase with the encumbrance, or what can be done to remove it.

Equity: The value of a homeowner's unencumbered interest in real estate. Equity is computed by subtracting from the property's fair market value the total of the unpaid mortgage balance and any outstanding liens or other debts against the property. A homeowner's equity increases as the mortgage is paid off, or as the property appreciates in value. When the mortgage and all other debts against the property are paid in full, the homeowner has 100% equity in the property.

Escheat: The reverting of property to the state due to failure of persons legally entitled to hold, or when heirs capable of inheriting are lacking the ability to do so.

Escrow: Funds paid by one party to another (the escrow agent) to hold until the occurrence of a specified event, after which the funds are released to a designated individual. In FHA mortgage transactions, an escrow account usually refers to the funds a mortgagor pays the lender at the time of the periodic mortgage payments. The money is held in a trust fund, provided by the lender for the buyer. Such funds should be adequate to cover yearly anticipated expenditures for mortgage insurance premiums, taxes, hazard insurance premiums, and special assessments.

Estate: The degree, quantum, nature, and extent of interest that one has in real property.

Execute: To perform what is required to give validity to a legal document. To execute a document, for example, means to sign it so that it becomes fully enforceable by law.

Fee Simple: The largest estate a person can have in real estate. Denotes totality of ownership, unlimited in point of time, as in perpetual.

Fiduciary: A person to whom property is entrusted; a trustee who holds, controls, or manages for another. A real estate agent is said to have a fiduciary responsibility and relationship with a client.

Foreclosure: A legal term applied to any of the various methods of enforcing payment of the debt secured by a mortgage, or deed of trust, by taking and selling the mortgaged property, and depriving the mortgagor of possession.

Forfeiture Clause: A clause in a lease enabling the landlord to terminate the lease and remove a tenant when the latter defaults in payment of rent or any other obligation under the lease.

Functional Obsolescence: An impairment of desirability of any property arising from its being out of date with respect to design and style, capacity and utility in relation to site, lack of modern facilities, and the like.

General Warranty Deed: A deed that conveys not only all the grantor's interests in and title to the property to the grantee, but also warrants that if the title is defective or has a "cloud" on it (such as mortgage claims, tax liens, title claims, judgments, or mechanic's liens against it) the grantee may hold the grantor liable.

Generally Accepted Accounting Principles (GAAP): A standardized set of accounting principles and concepts by which financial statements are prepared.

Grantee: That party in the deed who is the buyer or recipient; the person to whom the real estate is conveyed.

Grantor: That party in the deed who is the seller or giver; the person who conveys the real estate.

Hazard Insurance: Protects against damages caused to property by fire, wind- storms, and other common hazards.

Highest and Best Use: That use of, or program of utilization of, a site that will produce the maximum net land returns over the total period comprising the future; the optimum use for a site.

Implied Warranty or Covenant: A guaranty of assurance the law supplies in an agreement, even though the agreement itself does not express the guaranty or assurance.

Income Statement: The financial report that summarizes a business's performance over a specific period of time.

Injunction: A writ or order of the court to restrain one or more parties to a suit from committing an inequitable or unjust act regarding the rights of some other party in the suit or proceeding.

Interest: A charge paid for borrowing money.

Internal Rate of Return (IRR) Method: A method of ranking an investment proposal using the rate of return on an investment, calculated by finding the discount rate that equates the present value of future cash inflows to the project's cost.

Joint Tenancy: Property held by two or more persons together with the right of survivorship. While the doctrine of survivorship has been abolished with respect to most joint tenancies, the tenancy by the entirety retains the doctrine of survivorship in content.

Judgment: The decision or sentence of a court of law as the result of proceedings instituted therein for the redress of an injury. A judgment declaring that one individual is indebted to another individual when properly docketed creates a lien on the real property of the judgment debtor.

Lease: A species of contract, written or oral, between the owner of real estate, the landlord, and another person, the tenant, covering the conditions upon which the tenant may possess, occupy, and use the real estate.

Lessee: A person who leases property from another person, usually the landlord.

Lessor: The owner or person who rents or leases property to a tenant or lessee; the landlord.

Liabilities The debts of a business or entity in the form of financial claims on its assets.

LIBOR (London Interbank Offered Rate): The interest rate charged among banks in the foreign market for short-term loans to one another. A common index for ARM loans.

Lien: A claim by one person on the property of another as security for money owed. Such claims may include obligations not met or satisfied, judgments, unpaid taxes, materials, or labor.

Limited Liability Partnership (Limited Liability Company): A hybrid form of organization in which all partners enjoy limited liability for the business's debts. It combines the limited liability advantage of a corporation with the tax advantages of a partnership.

Limited Partnership: A hybrid form of organization consisting of general partners who have unlimited liability for the partnership's debts, and limited partners, whose liability is limited to the amount of their investment.

Loan Application: An initial statement of personal and financial information required to apply for a loan.

Loan Application Fee: Fee charged by a lender to cover the initial costs of processing a loan application. The fee may include the cost of obtaining a property appraisal, a credit report, and a lock-in fee or other closing costs incurred during the process, or the fee may be in addition to these charges.

Loan Origination Fee: Fee charged by a lender to cover administrative costs of processing a loan.

Loan-to-Value Ratio (LTV): The percentage of the loan amount to the appraised value (or the sales price, whichever is less) of the property.

Lock or Lock-In: A lender's guarantee of an interest rate for a set period of time. The period is usually that between loan application approval and loan closing. The lock-in protects you against rate increases during that time.

Market Value: The amount a property would sell for if put on the open market and sold in the manner property is ordinarily sold in the community in which the property is situated. The highest price estimated in terms of money that a buyer would be warranted in paying and a seller would be justified in accepting, provided both parties were fully informed, acted intelligently and voluntarily, and furthermore that all the rights and benefits inherent in or attributable to the property were included in the transfer.

Marketable Title: A title that is free and clear of objectionable liens, clouds, or other title defects. A title that enables an owner to sell the property freely to others, and which others will accept without objection.

Meeting of Minds: A mutual intention of two persons to enter into a contract affecting their legal status based on agreed upon terms.

Metes and Bounds: A term that comes from the old English words "metes," meaning measurements, and "bounds," meaning boundaries. It is generally applied to any description of real estate; describes the boundaries by distance and angles.

Mortgage: A lien or claim against real property given by the buyer to the lender as security for money borrowed. Under government-insured or loan guarantee provisions, the payments may include escrow amounts covering taxes, hazard insurance, water charges, and special assessments. Mortgages generally run from 10 to 30 years, during which the loan is to be paid in full.

Mortgage Commitment: A written notice from the bank or other lending institution saying it will advance mortgage funds in a specified amount to enable a buyer to purchase a house.

Mortgage Note: A written agreement to repay a loan. The agreement is secured by a mortgage, serves as proof of an indebtedness, and states the manner in which it shall be paid. The note states the actual amount of the debt that the mortgage secures and renders the mortgagor personally responsible for repayment.

Mortgage (Open End): A mortgage with a provision that permits borrowing additional money in the future without refinancing the loan or paying additional financing charges. Open-end provisions often limit such borrowing to no more than would raise the balance to the original loan figure.

Mortgagee: The lender in a mortgage agreement.

Mortgagor: The borrower in a mortgage agreement.

Net Cash Flow: The actual net cash, as opposed to accounting net income, that a firm generates during some specified period.

Net Income: In general, synonymous with net earnings, but considered a broader and better term; the balance remaining after deducting from the gross income all expenses, maintenance, taxes, and losses pertaining to operating properties except for interest or other financial charges on borrowed or other forms of capital.

Net Lease: A lease where, in addition to the rent stipulated, the lessee assumes payment of all property charges such as taxes, insurance, and maintenance.

Nonconforming Use: A use of land that predates zoning, but which is not

In accordance with the uses prescribed for the area by the zoning ordinance. Because it was there first, it may be continued, subject to certain limitations.

Note: An instrument of credit given to attest a debt; a written promise to pay money, which may or may not accompany a mortgage or other security agreement.

Offer: A proposal, oral or written, to buy a piece of property at a specified price under specified terms and conditions.

Option: The exclusive right to purchase or lease a property at a stipulated price or rent within a specified period of time.

Percentage Lease: A lease of commercial property in which the rent is computed as a percentage of the receipts, either gross or net, from the business being conducted by the lessee, sometimes with a guaranteed minimum rental.

Personal Property: Moveable property that is not by definition real property, including tangible property such as moneys, goods, chattel, as well as debts and claims.

Planned Unit Development (PUD): Residential complex of mixed housing types. Offers greater design flexibility than traditional developments. PUDs permit clustering of homes, sometimes not allowed under standard zoning ordinances, utilization of open space, and a project harmonious with the natural topography of the land.

Points: Sometimes referred to as 'discount points.' A point is one percent of the amount of the mortgage loan. For example, if a loan is for $250,000, one point is $2,500. Points are charged by a lender to raise the yield on a loan at a time when money is tight, interest rates are high, and there is a legal limit to the interest rate that can be charged on a mortgage. Buyers are prohibited from paying points on HUD or Veterans' Administration guaranteed loans (sellers can pay them, however). On a conventional mortgage, points may be paid by either buyer or seller or split between them.

Portfolio: The combined holdings of more than one stock, bond, real estate asset, or another asset by an investor.

Prepayment: Payment of mortgage loan, or part of it, before due date. Mortgage agreements often restrict the right of prepayment either by limiting the amount that can be prepaid in any one year or charging a penalty for prepayment. The Federal Housing Administration does not permit such restrictions in FHA insured mortgages.

Principal: The basic element of the loan as distinguished from interest and mortgage insurance premium. In other words, principal is the amount upon which interest is paid. The word also means one who appoints an agent to act for, and in behalf of, the person bound by an agent's authorized contract.

Property: The term used to describe the rights and interests a person has in lands, chattel, and other determinate things.

Purchase Agreement: An offer to purchase that has been accepted by the seller and has become a binding contract.

Quiet Enjoyment: The right of an owner of an interest in land, whether an owner or a tenant, to protection against disturbance or interference with possession of the land.

Quitclaim Deed: A deed that transfers whatever interest the maker of the deed may have in the particular parcel of land. A quitclaim deed is often given to clear the title when the grantor's interest in a property is questionable. By accepting such a deed, the buyer assumes all the risks.

Such a deed makes no warranties as to the title, but simply transfers to the buyer whatever interest the grantor has. (*See* deed.)

Real Estate Agent: An intermediary who buys and sells real estate for a company, firm, or individual and is compensated on a commission basis. The agent does not have title to the property, but generally represents the owner.

Real Estate Investment Trust (REIT): An entity that allows a very large number of investors to participate in the purchase of real estate, but as passive investors. The investors do not buy directly, but instead purchase shares in the REIT that owns the real estate investment. REITs are fairly common with the advent of mutual funds and can be purchased for as little as $10 per share and sometimes less.

Real Property: Land and buildings and anything that may be permanently attached to them.

Recording: The placing of a copy of a document in the proper books in the office of the Register of Deeds so that a public record will be made of it.

Redemption: The right that an owner-mortgagor, or one claiming under him or her, has after execution of the mortgage to recover back the title to the mortgaged property by paying the mortgage debt, plus interest and any other costs or penalties imposed, prior to the occurrence of a valid foreclosure. The payment discharges the mortgage and places the title back as it was at the time the mortgage was executed.

Refinancing: The process of the same mortgagor paying off one loan with the proceeds from another loan.

Reformation: The correction of a deed or other instrument by reason of a mutual mistake of the parties involved, or because of the mistake of one party caused by the fraud or inequitable conduct of the other party.

Release: The giving up or abandoning of a claim or right to the person against whom the claim exists or against whom the right is to be exercised or enforced.

Release of Lien: The discharge of certain property from the lien of a judgment, mortgage, or claim.

Renewal: Taking a new lease after an existing lease expires.

Rent: A compensation, either in money, provisions, chattel, or labor, received by the owner from a tenant for the occupancy of the premises.

Rescission of Contract: The abrogating or annulling of a contract; the revocation or repealing of a contract by mutual consent of the parties to the contract, or for other causes as recognized by law.

Restrictive Covenants: Private restrictions limiting the use of real property. Restrictive covenants are created by deed and may run with the land, thereby binding all subsequent purchasers of the land, or may be deemed personal and binding only between the original seller and buyer. The determination whether a covenant runs with the land or is personal is governed by the language of the covenant, the intent of the parties, and the law in the state where the land is situated. Restrictive covenants that run with the land are encumbrances and may affect the value and marketability of title. Restrictive covenants may limit the density of buildings per acre, regulate size, style, or price range of buildings to be erected, or prevent particular businesses from operating or minority groups from owning or occupying homes in a given area. This latter discriminatory covenant is unconstitutional and has been declared unenforceable by the U.S. Supreme Court.

Retained Earnings: That portion of a firm's earnings that has been saved rather than paid out as dividends.

Retained Earnings: That portion of the firm's earnings that has been saved rather than paid out as dividends.

Return on Assets (ROA): The ratio of net income to total assets.

Return on Equity (ROE): The ratio of net income to equity; measures the rate of return on common stockholders' investment.

Revocation: The recall of a power or authority conferred, or the vacating of an instrument previously made.

Right of Survivorship: Granted to two joint owners who purchase using that buying method. Stipulates that one gets full rights and becomes the sole owner of the property upon the death of the other. Right of survivorship is the fundamental difference between acquiring property as joint owners and as tenants in common.

Sales Agreement. (See agreement of sale)

Security Deposit: Money or things of value received by or for a property owner to ensure payment of rent and the satisfactory condition of the rented premises upon termination of the written or oral lease.

Security Interest: An interest in property that secures payment or performance of an obligation.

Special Assessment: A legal charge against real estate by a public authority to pay the cost of public improvements, such as for the opening, grading, and guttering of streets, the construction of sidewalks and sewers, or the installation of street lights or other such items to be used for public purposes.

Special Lien: A lien that binds a specified piece of property, unlike a usual or general lien, which is levied against all one's assets. It creates a right to retain something of value belonging to another person as compensation for labor, material, or money expended in that person's behalf. In some localities, it is called 'particular' lien or 'specific' lien. (*See* lien.)

Special Warranty Deed: A deed in which the grantor conveys title to the grantee and agrees to protect the grantee against title defects or claims asserted by the grantor and those persons whose right to assert a claim against the title arose during the period the grantor held title to the property. In a special warranty deed, the grantor guarantees to the grantee that nothing has been done during the time title to the property was held that has, or which might in the future, impair the grantee's title.

Specific Performance: A remedy in court of equity whereby the defendant may be compelled to do whatever was agreed to in a contract executed by the defendant.

Statute: A law established by the act of the legislative powers; an act of the legislature; the written will of the legislature solemnly expressed according to the forms necessary to constitute it as the law provides.

Subdivision: A tract of land divided into smaller parcels of land, or lots, usually for constructing new houses.

Sublease: An agreement whereby one person who has leased land from the owner rents out all or a portion of the premises for a period ending prior to the expiration of the original lease.

Subordination Clause: A clause in a mortgage or lease stating that one who has a prior claim or interest agrees that this interest or claim shall be secondary or subordinate to a subsequent claim, encumbrance, or interest.

Survey: A map or plat made by a licensed surveyor showing the results of measuring the land with its elevations, improvements, boundaries, and its relationship to surrounding tracts of land. A survey is often required by the lender to assure that a building is actually sited on the land according to its legal description.

Survivorship: The distinguishing feature of a tenancy by the entirety, by which on the death of one spouse, the surviving spouse acquires full ownership.

Tax: As applied to real estate, an enforced charge imposed on persons, property, or income, to be used to support the State. The governing body in turn utilizes the funds in the best interest of the general public.

Tax Deed: A deed given where property has been purchased at public sale because of the owner's nonpayment of taxes.

Tax Sale: A sale of property for nonpayment of taxes assessed against it.

Tenancy at Will: An arrangement under which a tenant occupies land with the consent of the owner, but without a definite termination date and without any definite agreement for regular payment of rent.

Tenancy in Common: Style of ownership in which two or more persons purchase a property jointly, but with no right of survivorship. Each tenant in common is the owner of an undivided fractional interest in the whole property. They are free to will their share to anyone they choose, a primary difference between that form of ownership and joint tenancy.

Tenant: One who holds or possesses land or tenements by any kind of title, either in fee, for life, for years, or at will. The term is most commonly used as one who has under lease the temporary use and occupation of real property that belongs to another person or persons. The tenant is the lessee.

Time is of the Essence: A phrase meaning that time is of crucial value and vital importance and that failure to fulfill time deadlines will be considered a failure to perform the contract.

Title: As generally used, the rights of ownership and possession of a particular property. In real estate usage, title may refer to the instruments or documents by which a right of ownership is established (title documents), or it may refer to the ownership interest one has in the real estate.

Title Insurance: Protects lenders or homeowners against loss of their interest in property due to legal defects in title. Title insurance may be issued to a mortgagee's title policy. Insurance benefits will be paid only to the 'named insured' in the title policy, so it is important that an owner purchase an 'owner's title policy' if he or she desires the protection of title insurance.

Title Search or Examination: A check of the title records, generally at the local courthouse, to make sure the buyer is purchasing a house from the legal owner and there are no liens, overdue special assessments, or other claims or outstanding restrictive covenants filed in the record that would adversely affect the marketability or value of title.

Trust: A relationship under which one person, the trustee, holds legal title to property for the benefit of another person, the trust beneficiary.

Trustee: A party who is given legal responsibility to hold property in the best interest of or 'for the benefit of' another. The trustee is one placed in a position of responsibility for another, a responsibility enforceable in a court of law. (*See* deed of trust.)

Truth-in-lending Act: Federal law requiring written disclosure of the terms of a mortgage (including the APR and other charges) by a lender to a borrower after application. Also requires the right to rescission period.

Underwriting: In mortgage lending, the process of determining the risks involved in and establishing suitable terms and conditions for the loan.

Unimproved: As relating to land, vacant or lacking in essential appurtenant improvements required to serve a useful purpose.

Useful life: The period over which a commercial property can be depreciated for tax purposes. A property's useful life is also referred to as its economic life.

Usury: Charging a higher rate of interest on a loan than is allowed by law.

Valid: Having force, or binding forces; legally sufficient and authorized by law.

Valuation: The act or process of estimating value; the amount of estimated value.

Value: Ability to command goods, including money, in exchange; the quantity of goods, including money, that should be commanded or received in exchange for the item valued. As applied to real estate, value is the present worth of all the rights to future benefits arising from ownership.

Variance: An exception to a zoning ordinance granted to meet certain specific needs, usually given on an individual case-by-case basis.

Void: That which is unenforceable; having no force or effect.

Waiver: Renunciation, disclaiming, or surrender of some claim, right, or prerogative.

Warranty Deed: A deed that transfers ownership of real property and in which the grantor guarantees that the title is free and clear of all encumbrances.

Zoning Ordinances: The acts of an authorized local government establishing building codes and setting forth regulations for property land usage.

About the Author

As the owner of Kahuna Investments, Corey Peterson strives to provide his investors with stable cash flow returns and long-term capital appreciation by buying multi-family apartments. In addition to apartments, he has flipped, acquired and sold over $49 million in real estate across the country. He has also been involved in the ownership and management of more than $31 Million dollars' worth of commercial properties nationwide and is frequently asked to speak on this subject, including at Harvard University. Corey is also the host of the podcast, Multi-Family Legacy Podcast and has been featured on FOX, CBS, ABC, and NBC affiliates.

Corey holds many certifications in real estate strategies and belongs to several networking groups. This includes his own REIA, the East Valley Investors Club. In addition, he runs a mastermind group called the Big Kahuna Club. This group brings local business owners together to discuss current business practices and what's working in the local economy. Finally, Corey is a member of Arizona Multi-Family Association, Arizona

Real Estate Investing Association, and Independent Rental Owners Council.

Business is not everything. Corey serves as a member of Rotary International and has hosted several foreign exchange students at his home. Furthermore, Corey donates his time to Junior Achievement, where he teaches high school students. In a 10-week program, these young people learn entrepreneurial skills and focus on creating a business and developing products to bring to market.

To learn more about how Corey can help you get massive cash flow to your investors by buying apartment buildings, contact him directly at Corey@KahunaInvestments.com, or visit his website to learn more about his services at **www.KahunaInvestments.com**.

Made in the
USA
Middletown, DE